THE MILDEST HERALD BY OUR FATE ALLOTTED
BECKONS, AND WITH INVERTED TORCH DOTH STAND
TO LEAD US WITH A GENTLE HAND
INTO THE LAND OF THE DEAR DEPARTED,
INTO THE SILENT LAND!"

VOICES

FROM

THE SILENT LAND;

OR,

LEAVES OF CONSOLATION FOR THE AFFLICTED.

BY

MRS. H. DWIGHT WILLIAMS.

O, soothe us, haunt us, night and day,
Ye gentle spirits far away,
With whom we shared the cup of grace,
Then parted — ye to Christ's embrace,
We to the lonesome world again;
Yet mindful of th' unearthly strain
Practised with you at Eden's door,
To be sung on, where angels soar,
With blended voices evermore.

KEBLE.

BOSTON:
PUBLISHED BY JOHN P. JEWETT AND COMPANY.
CLEVELAND, OHIO:
JEWETT, PROCTOR, AND WORTHINGTON.
LONDON: LOW AND COMPANY.
1858.

STEREOTYPED AT THE
BOSTON STEREOTYPE FOUNDRY.

METCALF AND COMPANY,
PRINTERS TO THE UNIVERSITY.

DEDICATED

TO

The Memory of One

WHO HAS DEPARTED TO

THE SILENT LAND;

A MUCH-LOVED AND DEEPLY-LAMENTED BROTHER, WHOSE
EARLY AND IRREPARABLE LOSS HAS CAUSED
THE GATHERING OF THESE

LEAVES OF CONSOLATION.

"Why, he but sleeps:
If he be gone, he'll make his grave a bed.
. . . . .
With fairest flowers,
I'll sweeten thy sad grave. Thou shalt not lack
The flower that's like thy face, pale primrose, nor
The azured harebell, like thy veins; no, nor
The leaf of eglantine, whom not to slander,
Outsweetened not thy breath; the redbreast would,
With charitable bill, bring thee all this;
Yea, and furred moss besides, when flowers are none
To winterground thy corse."

PREFACE.

"INTO the Silent Land!" Ah, who can say that the footsteps of none he once loved on earth have entered the "shadows of that pale realm"? Death, sooner or later, cometh to all: the white and venerable locks of the aged, the maturity of manhood, the ruddy freshness of youth, whose flashing eye is salient with life and health, and the tender bud of infancy, — all soon, too soon, fall before the scythe of the pitiless destroyer.

> "The air is full of farewells to the dying,
> And mournings for the dead."

No suffering, no anguish, is like unto that of the deeply heart-stricken mourner, as he bendeth over his forever-hushed, but beloved, dead. Often, at such times, the heart and soul, though wonderfully stirred, feels a grief "too deep for tears." A link of the chain that bound him to earth has been rudely riven; and the vanity of this life, the nearness of eternity, with its all-absorbing interests, are felt and acknowledged. Such sad visitations of Providence induce within us an insatiable desire to know more of the future; and the flight thitherward of the spirit of one who in life has been very dear, perhaps the dearest, seems to cast a soft halo of light into that future. Then the Christian finds the blessed promises of God, and the death and resurrection of Christ, unspeakably precious; he feels the need of the heavenly Comforter, and, while seeking to cast all his care on him, "knowing that he careth for him," what may have seemed the dark and distant future is illumed with an almost unclouded noonday brightness. Every earthly woe, every trial and care, can be mitigated by the consoling and sustaining influences of our holy religion. God has promised to "comfort all who mourn," if, in the time of their sorrow, they seek him.

Prayer, and reading the word of God, will not only afford sweet consolation in the deepest affliction, but prove a tower of defence, a shield against the temptations that frequently assail us at such times. Another source of comfort is to be found in the perusal of the writings of good and holy men who have felt the same bitter heart grief, and whose works abound with passages most touchingly fitted to console under the heaviest afflictions; teaching us how to meet, bear, and wisely use all such chastenings for our spiritual advancement. Our literature, too, contains much prose and poetry addressed to the heart stricken, desponding, and desolate, who, in times of bereavement, love to linger among the "graves of their household," and dwell upon the state of the departed.

These "Voices from the Silent Land" have been collected in the freshness of a very deep affliction, and completed before its daily-gushing anguish had passed away. The compiler's aim and object is to induce some to make a good and wise use of afflictive dispensations, to see the hand of God in them all, and to feel that "the Judge of all the earth will do right." She can only desire that the perusal of these pages may prove as sweet and soothing a source of consolation to others as their preparation has been to herself. The women of the United States, however elevated and affluent their station, are rarely *entirely* free from the perplexities and anxieties of domestic cares, and can seldom find sufficient leisure to peruse or examine all the works from which this volume has been gathered; therefore it is designed more particularly for my countrywomen whom God, in infinite wisdom, may have caused to pass under the rod of affliction, but who, I trust, can say, with the poet, —

> "'Tis sweet, as year by year we lose
> Friends out of sight, in faith to muse
> How grows in paradise our store."

M. N. W.

May 10, 1851.

CONTENTS.

NOTE.

The compiler would express her grateful acknowledgments to Mrs. Julia Norton, Messrs. W. C. Bryant, H. W. Longfellow, N. P. Willis, Park Benjamin, Charles Sprague, and James T. Fields, for kindly granting her permission to publish the articles, which appear in this volume, from their pens.

THE SILENT LAND.

DEATH.

BERNARD BARTON.

It is when death and darkness come, men learn, if not before, what their nature is; to what it is exposed, and by what sustained; what it needs and craves. The future and eternity are made sure. They are brought close around them. They have an interest there now; they have treasure there. A part of themselves is there. The parent who gave them being; the brother or sister who shared that being; the child who was all their own, is there — and *they* are there also. Their nature, all their affections, were reposed in those objects; and you cannot, no power can change — death, worlds, cannot sever them wholly. Their very removal to an unknown state makes that state known. Their flight into the distant and dark future illumes that future. The angel of death, who bore the loved away, opened the heavens as he ascended; and now the eye of faith penetrates, the heart of faith lives, in that spiritual world. There is sorrow and trembling yet. But there is hope, the anchor of the soul. There is faith, the very substance of things hoped for, the evidence of things not seen.

There is prayer and communion, the soul's pinions, on which it soars to the bright presence of the spirits it here loved, the Savior whom it trusts, the Father in whom it dwells. From the region and shadow of death, light is sprung up. It is the light of God's countenance; it irradiates the features, the souls, with which we have been long familiar—with which we may now live forever.

THE DEAD ARE EVERY WHERE.

ANON.

THE dead are every where!
The mountain side, the plain, the wood profound,
All the wide earth, the fertile and the fair,
Is one vast burial ground!

Within the populous streets,
In solitary homes, in places high,
In pleasure domes, where pomp and luxury meet,
Men bow themselves to die.

The old man at his door,
The unweaned child, murmuring his wordless song,
The bondman and the free, the rich, the poor,
All—all to death belong!

The sunlight gilds the walls
Of kingly sepulchres, inwrought with brass;

And the long shadow of the cypress falls
Athwart the common grass.

The living of gone time
Builded their glorious cities by the sea ;
And, awful in their greatness, sat sublime,
As if no change could be.

There was the eloquent tongue ;
The poet's heart, the sage's soul was there ;
And loving women, with their children young,
The faithful and the fair.

They were, but they are not.
Suns rose and set, and earth put on her bloom ;
Whilst man, submitting to the common lot,
Went down into the tomb.

And still amid the wrecks
Of mighty generations passed away,
Earth's honest growth, the fragrant wild flower, decks
The tomb of yesterday.

And in the twilight deep,
Go veiléd women forth, like her who went —
Sister of Lazarus — to the grave to weep,
To breathe in low lament.

The dead are every where !
Where'er is love, or tenderness, or faith ;
Where'er is pleasure, pomp, or pride ; where'er
Life is or was, is death !

BLESSED ARE THE DEAD.

SIMON DACH.

O, HOW blessed are ye whose toils are ended!
Who, through death, have unto God ascended!
Ye have arisen
From the cares which keep us still in prison.

We are still as in a dungeon living,
Still oppressed with sorrow and misgiving;
Our undertakings
Are but toils, and troubles, and heart-breakings.

Ye, meanwhile, are in your chambers sleeping,
Quiet, and set free from all our weeping;
No cross nor trial
Hinders your enjoyments with denial.

Christ has wiped away your tears forever;
Ye have that for which we still endeavor.
To you are chanted
Songs which yet no mortal ear have haunted.

Ah, who would not, then, depart with gladness,
To inherit heaven for earthly sadness?
Who here would languish
Longer in bewailing and in anguish?

Come, O Christ, and loose the chains that bind us;
Lead us forth, and cast this world behind us.
With thee, th' Anointed,
Finds the soul its joy and rest appointed.

DUTY OF COMFORTING THE AFFLICTED.

JEREMY TAYLOR.

CERTAIN it is, that as nothing can better do it, so there is nothing greater, for which God made our tongues, next to reciting his praises, than to minister comfort to a weary soul. And what greater measure can we have than that we should bring joy to our brother, who, with his dreary eyes, looks to heaven and round about, and cannot find so much rest as to lay his eyelids close together — than that thy tongue should be tuned with heavenly accents, and make the weary soul to listen for light and ease; and when he perceives that there is such a thing in the world, and in the order of things, as comfort and joy, to begin to break out from the prison of his sorrows at the door of sighs and tears, and by little and little melt into showers and refreshment? This is glory to thy voice, and employment fit for the brightest angel. But so have I seen the sun kiss the frozen earth, which was bound up with the images of death, and the colder breath of the north; and then the waters break from their enclosures, and melt with joy, and run in useful channels; and the flies do rise again from their little graves in walls, and dance a while in the air, to tell that there is joy within, and that the great mother of creatures will open the stock of her new refreshment, become useful to mankind, and sing praises to her Redeemer. So is the heart of a sorrowful man under the discourses of a wise comforter; he breaks from the despairs of the grave, and the fetters and chains of sorrow; he blesses God, and he blesses thee, and he feels his life returning; for to be miserable is death, but nothing is life but to be comforted; and God is pleased with no music from below so much as in the thanksgiving songs of relieved widows, of supported orphans, of rejoicing, and comforted, and thankful persons.

"Whom the Lord loveth he chasteneth, and scourgeth every son whom he receiveth. If ye endure chastening, God dealeth with you as with sons; for what son is he whom the father chasteneth not?"—HEBREWS xii.

THE HOUR OF DEATH.

MRS. HEMANS.

LEAVES have their time to fall,
And flowers to wither at the north wind's breath
And stars to set—but all,
Thou hast *all* seasons for thine own, O Death!

Day is for mortal care;
Eve, for glad meetings round the joyous hearth;

Night, for the dreams of sleep, the voice of prayer—
But all for thee, thou mightiest of the earth.

The banquet hath its hour—
Its feverish hour—of mirth, and song, and wine;
There comes a day for grief's o'erwhelming power,
A time for softer tears—but all are thine.

Youth and the opening rose
May look like things too glorious for decay,
And smile at thee—but thou art not of those
That wait the ripened bloom to seize their prey.

Leaves have their time to fall,
And flowers to wither at the north wind's breath,
And stars to set—but all,
Thou hast *all* seasons for thine own, O Death!

We know when moons shall wane,
When summer birds from far shall cross the sea,
When autumn's hue shall tinge the golden grain—
But who shall teach us when to look for thee?

Is it when Spring's first gale
Comes forth to whisper where the violets lie?
Is it when roses in our paths grow pale?—
They have *one* season—*all* are ours to die.

Thou art where billows foam;
Thou art where music melts upon the air;
Thou art around us in our peaceful home;
And the world calls us forth—and thou art there.

Thou art where friend meets friend,
Beneath the shadow of the elm to rest;
Thou art where foe meets foe, and trumpets rend
The skies, and swords beat down the princely crest.

Leaves have their time to fall,
And flowers to wither at the north wind's breath,
And stars to set — but all,
Thou hast *all* seasons for thine own, O Death!

"It is not the design or plan of God — his nature will not allow of any such design or plan — to deprive his creatures of happiness, but only to pour the cup of bitterness into all that happiness, and smite all that joy and prosperity which the creature has in any thing *out of Himself*." — FENELON.

WHAT IS DEATH?

REV. GEORGE CROLEY.

WHAT is death? 'tis to be free;
No more to love, or hope, or fear;
To join the dread equality;
All, all alike are humble there.
The mighty wave
Wraps lord and slave.
Nor pride, nor poverty, dares come
Within that refuge house — the tomb.

Spirit with the drooping wing,
And the ever-weeping eye,
Thou of all earth's kings art king;
Empires at thy footstool lie.
Beneath thee strewed,
Their multitude
Sink like waves upon the shore;
Storms shall never rouse them more.

What's the grandeur of the earth
To the grandeur round thy throne?
Riches, glory, beauty, birth,
To thy kingdoms all have gone.
Before thee stand
The wondrous band—
Bards, heroes, sages, side by side—
Who darkened nations when they died. .

Earth hath hosts, but thou canst show
Many a million for her one.
Through thy gates the mortal flow
Has for countless years rolled on.
Back from the tomb
No step has come;
There fixed till the last thunder's sound
Shall bid thy prisoners be unbound.

DEATH A SLEEP.

REV. JOHN HARRIS.

So ample and sufficient are the preparatory measures which Christ has taken for the final extinction of death, that he speaks of it in terms of comparative disparagement and indifference. So effectually is it disarmed and mutilated, and so completely at the disposal of Christ, that he speaks of it already as if it were not. "Whosoever believeth in me shall never die." "If a man keep my sayings, he shall never taste of death; he shall never see death." In accordance with these representations, he has given the state of death the soft and tranquillizing name of *sleep*.

"For if we believe that Jesus died, and rose again, even so them also which sleep in Jesus will God bring with him."—1 THESSALONIANS iv.

DEATH AND SLEEP.

KRUMMACHER.

In brotherly embrace walked the Angel of Sleep and the Angel of Death upon the earth. It was evening. They laid themselves down upon a hill not far from the dwelling of men. A melancholy silence prevailed around, and the chimes of the evening bell, in the distant hamlet, ceased. Still and silent, as was their custom, sat these two beneficent genii of the human race, their arms entwined with cordial familiarity; and soon the shades of night gathered around them. Then arose the Angel of Sleep from his moss-grown couch, and strewed with a gentle hand the invisible grains of slumber. The evening breeze wafted them to the quiet dwelling of the tired husbandman, infolding in sweet sleep the inmates of the rural cottage, from the old man upon the staff down to the infant in the cradle. The sick forgot their pain; the mourners their grief; the poor their care. All eyes closed. His task accomplished, the benevolent Angel of Sleep laid himself again by the side of his grave brother. "When Aurora awakes," exclaimed he, with innocent joy, "men praise me as their friend and benefactor. O, what happiness, unseen and secretly, to confer such benefits! How blessed are we to be the invisible messengers of the Good Spirit! How beautiful is our silent calling!" So spake the friendly Angel of Slumber.

The Angel of Death sat with still deeper melancholy on his brow, and a tear, such as mortals shed, appeared in his large dark eyes. "Alas!" said he, "I may not, like thee, rejoice in the cheerful thanks of mankind; they call me, upon the earth, their enemy and joy killer." "O my brother," replied the gentle Angel of Slumber, "and will not the good man, at his awakening, recognize in thee his friend and benefactor, and gratefully bless thee in his joy? Are we not brothers, and ministers of one Father?" As he spoke, the eyes of the Death Angel beamed with pleasure, and again did the two friendly genii cordially embrace each other.

"HE GIVETH HIS BELOVED SLEEP."

BISHOP SPENCER.

I TREAD the churchyard's path alone,
  Unseen to shed the gushing tear;
I read on many a mouldering stone
  Fond records of the good and dear.
My soul is well nigh faint with fear,
  Where doubting Mary went to weep.
And yet what sweet repose is here —
  "He giveth his belovéd sleep."

The world is but a feverish rest,
  To weary pilgrims sometimes given,
When pleasure's cup has lost its zest,
  And glory's hard-earned crown is riven.

Here, softer than the dews of even
  Fall peaceful on the slumbering deep,
Asleep to earth, awake to heaven —
  " He giveth his belovéd sleep."

Yes, on the grave's hard pillow rise
  No cankering cares, no dreams of woe ;
On earth we close our aching eyes,
  And heavenward all our visions grow.
The airs of Eden round us flow,
  And in their balm our slumbers steep.
God calls his chosen home, and so
  " He giveth his belovéd sleep."

Ah ! vainly would the human voice,
  In this dull world of sin and folly,
Tell how the sainted dead rejoice
  In those high realms where joy is holy —
Where no dim shade of melancholy
  Beclouds the rest which angels keep ;
Where, peace and bliss united wholly,
  " He giveth his belovéd sleep."

If on that brow, so fair and young,
  Affliction trace an early furrow ;
If Hope's too dear delusive tongue
  Has broke its promise of to-morrow ; —
Seek not the world again, to borrow
  The deathful print its votaries reap.
Man gives his loved ones pain and sorrow,
  God " giveth his belovéd sleep."

3

THE DEATH BED.

THOMAS HOOD.

WE watched her breathing through the night,
  Her breathing soft and low,
As in her breast the wave of life
  Kept heaving to and fro.

So silently we seemed to speak,
  So slowly moved about,
As we had lent her half our powers
  To eke her being out.

Our very hopes belied our fears,
  Our fears our hopes belied;
We thought her dying when she slept,
  And sleeping when she died.

For when the morn came dim and sad,
  And chill with early showers,
Her quiet eyelids closed;—she had
  Another morn than ours.

"We spend our years as a tale *that is told.* The days of our years *are* threescore years and ten; and if, by reason of strength, *they be* fourscore years, yet *is* their strength labor and sorrow: for it is soon cut off, and we fly away."—PSALM XC.

MUSIC AT A DEATH BED.

MRS. HEMANS.

BRING music! stir the brooding air
With an ethereal breath;
Bring sounds, my struggling soul to bear
Up from the couch of death!

A voice, a flute, a dreamy lay,
Such as the southern breeze
Might waft, at golden fall of day,
O'er blue transparent seas?

O, no! not such: that lingering spell
Would lure me back to life,
When my weaned heart hath said farewell,
And passed the gates of strife.

Let not a sigh of human love
Blend with the song its tone!
Let no disturbing echo move
One that must die alone!

But pour a solemn breathing strain
Filled with the soul of prayer!
Let a life's conflict, fear, and pain,
And trembling hope, be there.

Deeper, yet deeper! in my thought
  Lies more prevailing sound,
A harmony intensely fraught
  With pleading more profound.

A passion unto music given,
  A sweet yet piercing cry,
A breaking heart's appeal to Heaven,
  A bright faith's victory.

Deeper! O, may no richer power
  Be in those notes enshrined?
Can all, which crowds on earth's last hour,
  No fuller language find?

Away, and hush the feeble song,
  And let the chord be stilled;
For in another land ere long
  My dream shall be fulfilled.

PRAISE IN TIMES OF AFFLICTION.

REV. H. MELVILL.

WAS it a strange preparation for the Mount of Olives and the Garden of Gethsemane, to commemorate the mercies and chant the praises of the most high God? Nay, it is recorded of Luther that, on receiving any discouraging news, he was wont to say, "Come, let us sing the forty-sixth psalm"—that psalm which commences with the words, "God is our refuge and strength, a very present help in trouble; therefore will not we fear, though the earth be removed, and though the mountains be carried into the midst of the sea." And it were well for us if, in seasons of trouble, we betook ourselves to praise, and not only to prayer. If we find ourselves in circumstances of difficulty, if dangers surround us, and duties seem too great for our strength, we almost naturally cry unto God, and entreat of him assistance and guardianship. And indeed we do right. God has made our receiving conditional on our asking; and we can never be too diligent in supplicating at his hands the supply of our many necessities. But ought we to confine ourselves to prayer, as though praise were out of place when mercies are needed, and only become us when they have just been received? Not so; praise is the best auxiliary to prayer; and he who most bears in mind what has been done for him by God, will be most emboldened to supplicate fresh gifts from above. We should recount God's mercies; we should call upon our souls, and all that is within us, to laud and magnify his name when summoned to face new trials, and encounter fresh dangers. Would it sound strange if, on approaching the chamber where the father of a family had just breathed his last, you heard voices mingling, not in a melancholy chant, but rather in one of lofty commemoration, such as might be taken from the Jewish Hallel, "The Lord hath been mindful of us; he will bless us; he will bless the house of Israel; he will bless the house of Aaron"? "The Lord is on my side: I will not fear what man can do unto me." Would you be disposed to say that the widow and the orphans, whose voices you recognized in the thankful anthem, were strangely employed? and that the utterances over the dead would have more fittingly been those of earnest petition unto God, of deep-drawn entreaty for the light of his countenance and the strength of his spirit? Nay, the widow and her orphans, if not actually praying the most effectual of prayers, would be thereby most effectually preparing themselves for praying unto God. If, now that their chief earthly stay is removed, they have to enter on a dark and dangerous path, they cannot do better than thus call to mind what the Almighty has proved himself to others and themselves. The anthem is the best prelude to the supplication; and their first step towards the Mount of Olives will be all the firmer, if, before they cry, "Hold thou up our goings in thy paths," they join in the song, "His merciful kindness is great towards us, and the truth of the Lord endureth forever; praise ye the Lord." . . . . Christ and his apostles "sang a hymn," ere "they went out into the Mount of Olives." What had music, cheerful and animated music, to do with so sad and solemn an occasion? Nay, there is music in heaven: they who stand on the "sea of glass mingled with fire" have "the harps of God" in their hands; "they sing the song of Moses, the servant of God, and the song of the Lamb." Why, then, should music ever be out of place with those whose affections are above?

It would not be out of place in the chamber of the dying believer. He has just received, through the holy mystery of the eucharist, the body and the blood of his blessed Redeemer. And now his own failing voice, and the voices of relatives and friends, join in chanting words the conclusion of the sacramental service: "Glory be to God on high, and on earth peace, good will towards men. We praise thee, we bless thee, we worship thee, we glorify thee, we give thanks to thee for thy great glory, O Lord God, heavenly King, God the Father Almighty." Wonder ye, that, when there was the option either to say or to sing, they chose the singing at such a moment? Nay, they all felt that they had a rough hill to climb; and they remembered that, when Christ and his apostles had finished their last supper, "they sang a hymn," and then "went out into the Mount of Olives."

REJOICING IN HEAVEN.

MARY HOWITT.

O SPIRIT, freed from bondage,
  Rejoice, thy work is done!
The weary world is 'neath thy feet,
  Thou brighter than the sun!

Awake, and breathe the living air
  Of our celestial clime!
Awake to love that knows no change,
  Thou who hast done with time!

Awake! lift up thy joyful eyes,—
  See, all heaven's host appears;
And be thou glad exceedingly,
  Thou who hast done with tears!

Awake! ascend. Thou art not now
  With those of mortal birth;
The living God hath touched thy lips,
  Thou who hast done with earth.

THE FAREWELL TO THE DEAD.

MRS. HEMANS.

    COME near. Ere yet the dust
Soil the bright paleness of the settled brow,
Look on your brother, and embrace him now
    In still and solemn trust.
Come near. Once more let kindred lips be pressed
On his cold cheek; then bear him to his rest.

    Look yet on this young face.
What shall the beauty, from amongst us gone,
Leave of its image, even where most it shone,
    Gladdening its hearth and race?
Dim grows the semblance on man's heart impressed.
Come near, and bear the beautiful to rest.

Ye weep — and it is well;
For tears befit earth's partings. Yesterday,
Song was upon the lips of this pale clay,
And sunshine seemed to dwell
Where'er he moved, the welcomed and the blessed.
Now gaze — and bear the silent unto rest.

Look yet on him whose eye
Meets yours no more in sadness or in mirth.
Was he not fair amidst the sons of earth —
The beings born to die?
But not where death has power may love be blessed.
Come near, and bear ye the beloved to rest.

How may the mother's heart
Dwell on her son, and dare to hope again?
The spring's rich promise hath been given in vain —
The lovely must depart.
Is *he* not gone, our brightest and our best?
Come near, and bear the early-called to rest.

Look on him. Is he laid
To slumber from the harvest or the chase? —
Too still and sad the smile upon his face;
Yet that, even that, must fade.
Death holds not long unchanged his fairest guest.
Come near, and bear the mortal to his rest.

His voice of mirth hath ceased
Amidst the vineyards. There is left no place
For him, whose dust receives your vain embrace,
At the gay bridal feast.

Earth must take earth to moulder on her breast.
Come near; weep o'er him;—bear him to his rest.

Yet mourn ye not as they
Whose spirit's light is quenched. For him the past
Is sealed. He may not fall; he may not cast
His birthright's hope away.
All is not *here* of our beloved and blessed—
Leave ye the sleeper with his God to rest!

AGAINST REPINING AT DEATH.

WILLIAM DRUMMOND.

ETERNAL things are raised far above the sphere of generation and corruption, where the first matter, like an ever-flowing and ebbing sea, with divers waves, but the same water, keepeth a restless and never-tiring current. What is below, in the universality of the kind, not in itself doth abide. Man a long line of years hath continued; this man, every hundred, is swept away.

This earth is as a table book, and men are the notes: the first are washen out, that new may be written in. They who forewent us did leave a room for us; and should we grieve to do the same to those who should come after us? Who, being suffered to see the exquisite rarities of an antiquary's cabinet, is grieved that the curtain be drawn, and to give place to new pilgrims? And when the Lord of this universe hath showed us the amazing wonders of his various frame, should we take it to heart when he thinketh time to dislodge? This is his unalterable and inevitable decree: as we had no part of our will in our entrance into this life, we should not presume to any in our leaving it, but soberly learn to will that which He wills, whose very will giveth being to all that it wills; and, reverencing the Orderer, not repine at the order and laws which, all-where and always, are so perfectly established, that who would essay to correct and amend any of them, he should either make them worse or desire things beyond the level of possibility.

MOURN NOT THE DEAD.

ELIZA COOK.

MOURN not the dead — shed not a tear
  Above the moss-stained sculptured stone,
But weep for those whose living woes
  Still yield the bitter, rending groan.

Grieve not to see the eyelids close
  In rest that has no fevered start;
Wish not to break the deep repose
  That curtains round the pulseless heart.

But keep thy pity for the eyes
  That pray for night, yet fear to sleep,
Lest wilder, sadder visions rise
  Than those o'er which they waking weep.

Mourn not the dead — 'tis they alone
  Who are the peaceful and the free;
The purest olive branch is known
  To twine about the cypress tree.

Crime, pride, and passion hold no more
  The willing or the struggling slave;
The throbbing pangs of love are o'er,
  And hatred dwells not in the grave.

The world may pour its venomed blame,
  And fiercely spurn the shroud-wrapped bier;
Some few may call upon the name,
  And sigh to meet a "dull, cold ear."

But vain the scorn that would offend,
  And vain the lips that would beguile;
The coldest foe, the warmest friend,
  Are mocked by Death's unchanging smile.

The only watchword that can tell
  Of peace and freedom won by all
Is echoed by the tolling bell,
  And traced upon the sable pall.

"The heart knows that it may sorrow; that no prohibition has been uttered to stifle the voice of woe. Rachel was not chid when she wept for her children; and that grief in itself is perfectly innocent, who shall deny, when we point to the Holy One, 'a man of sorrows, and acquainted with grief,' throughout the whole course of his visible abode among the sons of Adam? The stillness commanded is not that of apathy, or of indifference, or of forced acquiescence: it is a patient waiting for the promised crown, while bending under the predicted cross." — CHARLOTTE ELIZABETH.

BETTER TO LOSE TEMPORAL THAN SPIRITUAL MERCIES.

REV. THOMAS BROOKS.

THOU canst not tell how bad thy heart might have proved under the enjoyment of those near and dear mercies that thou now hast lost. In the winter men gird their clothes close about them, but in the summer they let them hang loose. In the winter of adversity many a Christian girds his heart close to God, to Christ, to godliness, to duties, who, in the summer of mercy, hangs loose from all.

Who can seriously consider this, and not hold his peace, even then when God takes a jewel out of his bosom? Heap all the sweetest contentments and most desirable enjoyments of this world upon a man, they will not make him a Christian; heap them upon a Christian, they will not make him a better Christian. Many a Christian hath been made worse by the good things of this world; but where is the Christian that hath been bettered by them? Therefore be quiet when God strips thee of them.

Get thy heart more affected with spiritual losses, and then thy soul will be less afflicted with temporal losses. Hast thou lost nothing of that presence of God that once thou hadst with thy spirit? Hast thou lost none of those warmings, meltings, quickenings, and cheerings that once thou hadst? Hast thou lost nothing of thy communion with God, nor of the joys of the Spirit, nor of that peace of conscience, that thou once enjoyedst? Hast thou lost none of that ground that once thou hadst got upon sin, Satan, and the world? Hast thou lost nothing of that holy vigor, and heavenly heat, that once thou hadst in thy heart? If thou hast not, — which would be a miracle, a wonder, — why dost thou complain of this or that temporal loss? For what is this but to complain of the loss of thy purse, when thy gold is safe? But if thou art a loser in spirituals, why dost thou not rather complain that thou hast lost thy God, than that thou hast lost thy gold? and that thou hast lost thy Christ, than that thou hast lost thy husband? and that thou hast lost thy peace, than that thou hast lost thy child? and that thou art a loser in spirituals, than that thou art a loser in temporals? Dost thou mourn over the body the soul hath left? Mourn rather over the soul that God hath forsaken, as Samuel did for Saul, (1 Sam. xv. 35.)

ON THE DEATH OF JOSEPH RODMAN DRAKE.

FITZ-GREENE HALLECK.

GREEN be the turf above thee,
Friend of my better days!
None knew thee but to love thee,
Nor named thee but to praise.

Tears fell, when thou wert dying,
From eyes unused to weep;
And long, where thou art lying,
Will tears the cold turf steep.

When hearts, whose truth was proven,
Like thine, are laid in earth,
There should a wreath be woven,
To tell the world their worth.

And I, who woke each morrow
To clasp thy hand in mine,
Who shared thy joy and sorrow,
Whose weal and woe were thine,—

It should be mine to braid it
Around thy faded brow;
But I've in vain essayed it,
And feel I cannot now.

While memory bids me weep thee,
 Nor thoughts nor words are free,
The grief is fixed too deeply,
 That mourns a man like thee.

DEATH NOT FORMIDABLE TO THE CHRISTIAN.

SAURIN.

DEATH has nothing that is formidable to the Christian. In the tomb of Jesus Christ are dissipated all the terrors which the tomb of nature presents. In the tomb of nature I perceive a gloomy night, which the eye is unable to penetrate; in the tomb of Jesus Christ I behold light and life. In the tomb of nature the punishment of sin stares me in the face; in the tomb of Jesus Christ I find the expiation of it. In the tomb of nature I read the fearful doom pronounced upon Adam, and upon all his miserable posterity, "Dust thou art, and unto dust thou shalt return," (Gen. iii. 19;) but in the tomb of Jesus Christ my tongue is loosed into this triumphant song of praise: "O death, where is thy sting? O grave, where is thy victory? . . . . Thanks be to God who giveth us the victory, through our Lord Jesus Christ." (1 Cor. xv. 55, 57.) "Through death he hath destroyed him that had the power of death, that is, the devil; that he might deliver them who, through fear of death, were all their lifetime subject to bondage."

DEATH NO LONGER THE KING OF TERRORS.

G. MOORE.

THE true believer always connects the moral attributes of Deity with his conceptions of divine power; and with him, therefore, providence is but another name for the Creator's faithfulness to his creatures. Throughout the wide universe, Faith beholds evidence that goodness regulates might; so that all her expectations are raptures, because all futurity, all eternity, can be nothing but the unfolding of love. Hence Death is no longer the king of terrors, with uplifted hand ready to strike the trembling heart, but like an angel at the bed of a slumbering child, fanning it to sleep with a lily plucked from paradise, and filling the soul with visions of heaven, by blending in brightness, before its eyes, the sweetest images of earthly beauty and affection.

HE HAS GONE TO HIS GOD.

ANDREWS NORTON.

HE has gone to his God ; he has gone to his home ;
No more amid peril and error to roam.
His eyes are no longer dim ;
His feet will no more falter ;
No grief can follow him ;
No pang his cheek can alter.

There are paleness, and weeping, and sighs below;
For our faith is faint, and our tears will flow.
But the harps of heaven are ringing ;
Glad angels come to greet him ;
And hymns of joy are singing,
While old friends press to meet him.

O, honored, beloved, to earth unconfined,
Thou hast soared on high, thou hast left us behind.
But our parting is not forever ;
We will follow thee by heaven's light,
Where the grave cannot dissever
The souls whom God will unite.

THE GRAVE.

JAMES MONTGOMERY.

THERE is a calm for those who weep,
A rest for weary pilgrims found:
They softly lie, and sweetly sleep,
Low in the ground.

The storm, that wrecks the wintry sky,
No more disturbs their deep repose
Than summer evening's latest sigh,
That shuts the rose.

I long to lay this painful head
And aching heart beneath the soil,
To slumber, in that dreamless bed,
From all my toil.

The grave, that never spoke before,
Hath found at length a tongue to chide;
O, listen! I will speak no more —
Be silent, pride!

Art thou a mourner? Hast thou known
The joy of innocent delights,
Endearing days forever flown,
And tranquil nights?

O, live! and deeply cherish still
  The sweet remembrance of the past;
Rely on Heaven's unchanging will
      For peace at last.

Though long of winds and waves the sport,
  Condemned in wretchedness to roam,
Live! thou shalt reach a sheltering port,
      A quiet home.

Seek the true treasure, seldom found,
  Of power the fiercest griefs to calm,
And soothe the bosom's deepest wound
      With heavenly balm.

Whate'er thy lot, where'er thou be,
  Confess thy folly — kiss the rod;
And in thy chastening sorrows see
      The hand of God.

A bruiséd reed he will not break;
  Afflictions all his children feel;
He wounds them for his mercy's sake —
      He wounds to heal.

Humbled beneath his mighty hand,
  Prostrate his providence adore:
'Tis done! arise! he bids thee stand,
      To fall no more.

Now, traveller, in the vale of tears,
  To realms of everlasting light,

Through time's dark wilderness of years,
Pursue thy flight.

There is a calm for those who weep,
A rest for weary pilgrims found;
And while the mouldering ashes sleep
Low in the ground,—

The soul, of origin divine,
God's glorious image freed from clay,
In heaven's eternal sphere shall shine
A star of day!

The sun is but a spark of fire,
A transient meteor in the sky;
The soul, immortal as its Sire,
SHALL NEVER DIE!

THE GRAVE.

JONES.

"MAN goeth to his long home;" to "the house appointed for all living." "There the wicked cease from troubling, and there the weary be at rest. There the prisoners rest together; they hear not the voice of the oppressor. The small and great are there; and the servant is free from his master."

As a flower of the field, so man springs up, grows, flourishes, and fades, and disappears. He may be cut off in the morning, or in the midst, of his days, or his existence may be prolonged to old age; but every step that he takes on earth is a step towards the grave. The day will come when the frail tenement shall be consigned to the dust. "I have said to corruption, Thou art my father; to the worm, Thou art my mother and my sister."

This world will soon be to me a mere nothing. I shall exist, but I shall be a stranger to the plans, cares, sorrows, and vicissitudes of my successors in this vale of tears. I shall soon be forgotten; and ages will revolve, and generation succeed generation, while this dust and ashes shall be mingled with the clods of the valley, and with the elements of nature. But while I meditate on what lies before me, let me not fail to gather substantial improvement from the subject. Lessons of piety are valuable lessons. While then I look upon the grave, let me learn the necessity of dying to the world, before I die in it. Let me be urged to lay up treasures for that state of being where there is no change and no end.

Is the grave to be ere long my dwelling? How, then, can I fix my heart on earthly things? The rich, and great, and wise, and powerful among men go down to the chambers of silence. "We brought nothing into this world, and it is certain we can carry nothing out. And having food and raiment, let us be therewith content." The shroud, the coffin, the bier, and the grave — these teach me the emptiness of the world, and the vanity and folly of ambition and avarice. I think of these, and the pageantry of the world melts from my view as a gilded shadow.

Is the grave to be ere long my dwelling? How can I regard pleasure and gratification as my chief good? How can I be anxious to adorn the body with fashion and finery? I think on the grave, and I am compelled to own that I act a most unworthy part if I allow, for a moment, the lust of the flesh, and the lust of the eyes, and the pride of life, to be my masters.

Is the grave to be ere long my dwelling? Then let me look to things that survive the desolation of the grave. The immaterial soul is to act its part in an imperishable world, where it will be rich or poor, glorious or degraded, happy or miserable, forever. The body shall slumber in the grave for a season, but the soul is immortal. It is, then, my wisdom to love, and seek, and esteem, and pursue those things which will never decay; over which death and the grave have no dominion; that I may be rich, and happy, yea, blessed forevermore.

. . . . .

O my soul! let me often meditate on the grave. There, indeed, thou wilt not enter; for when the frail dust lodges there, thou wilt be in another world. Let thy attention, then, be faithfully given to the gospel of Christ, to the great things of religion, that it may be well with thee. Strive to live more and more as one who is to live here only for a little time, and who is to live in another state forever. In the strength of divine grace rise more above the world;

rise more above the hostile power of flesh and blood; rise higher towards thy God and Savior, and things invisible; press nearer to them. Then thou mayst view the brevity of time, the decay of nature, and the triumph of the grave, with dignified serenity; for eternal life is thy inheritance.

O blessed and glorious God, the Author of all good, enable me not only to meditate on serious things, but also to profit by my meditations on them. Enable me, by the grace of thy Holy Spirit, so to believe and live, that I may go down to the grave in sure and certain hope of the resurrection to eternal life, through the mediation and intercession of Jesus Christ, our only Lord and Savior. Amen.

THE LANGUAGE OF A GRAVESTONE.

CHARLOTTE ELIZABETH.

"STOP," says the crumbling monument of by-gone generations,—"stop, passenger, and mark me. Here lies a brother of your race; I show you precisely where he was laid under the sod. Dig, now, even to the centre, in quest of the frame so fearfully and wonderfully made. Search, sift every handful of earth as you cast it forth, you shall not find a vestige of my charge. All is resolved into the parent element, beyond the power of your keenest investigation to separate or discern the one from the other. Yet read me again. Here lies that mortal; and hence he shall again come forth, in a moment, in the twinkling of an eye, at the last trump. What you toss around you is the corruptible that must put on incorruption; the mortal that must put on immortality. Go learn from my defaced surface a lesson of faith: 'Blessed are they which believe, yet see not.'"

HYMN OF THE CHURCHYARD.

JOHN BETHUNE.

AH me! this is a sad and silent city:
  Let me walk softly o'er it, and survey
Its grassy streets with melancholy pity.
  Where are its children? where their gleesome
      play?
Alas! their cradled rest is cold and deep,—
Their playthings are thrown by, and they asleep.

This is pale beauty's bourn: but where the beautiful
  Whom I have seen come forth at evening's hours,
Leading their aged friends, with feelings dutiful,
  Amid the wreaths of spring, to gather flowers?
Alas! no flowers are here but flowers of death,
And those who once were sweetest sleep beneath.

This is a populous place: but where the bustling,—
  The crowded buyers of the noisy mart,—

The lookers on, — the snowy garments rustling, —
  The money changers, — and the men of art?
Business, alas! hath stopped in mid career,
And none are anxious to resume it here.

This is the home of grandeur: where are they —
  The rich, the great, the glorious, and the wise?
Where are the trappings of the proud, the gay —
  The gaudy guise of human butterflies?
Alas! all lowly lies each lofty brow,
And the green sod dizens their beauty now.

This is a place of refuge and repose:
  Where are the poor, the old, the weary wight,
The scorned, the humble, and the man of woes,
  Who wept for morn, and sighed again for night?
Their sighs at last have ceased, and here they sleep
Beside their scorners, and forget to weep.

This is a place of gloom: where are the gloomy?
  The gloomy are not citizens of death:
Approach and look where the long grass is plumy;
  See them above; they are not found beneath;
For these low denizens, with artful wiles,
Nature, in flowers, contrives her mimic smiles.

This is a place of sorrow: friends have met
  And mingled tears o'er those who answered not.
And where are they whose eyelids then were wet?
  Alas! their griefs, their tears, are all forgot:
They, too, are landed in this silent city,
Where there is neither love, nor tears, nor pity.

This is a place of fear: the firmest eye
  Hath quailed to see its shadowy dreariness;
But Christian hope, and heavenly prospects high,
  And earthly cares, and nature's weariness,
Have made the timid pilgrim cease to fear,
And long to end his painful journey here.

CHOICE OF BURIAL-PLACE.

REV. HENRY MELVILL.

It is not a Christian thing to die manifesting indifference as to what is done with the body. That body is redeemed: not a particle of its dust but was bought with drops of Christ's precious blood. That body is appointed to a glorious condition: not a particle of the corruptible but what shall put on incorruption; of the mortal that shall not assume immortality. The Christian knows this; it is not the part of a Christian to seem unmindful of this. He may, therefore, as he departs, speak of the place where he would wish to be laid. "Let me sleep," he may say, "with my father and my mother, with my wife and my children: lay me not here, in this distant land, where my dust cannot mingle with its kindred. I would be chimed to my grave by my own village bell, and have my requiem sung where I was baptized in Christ." Marvel ye at such last words? Wonder ye that one whose spirit is just entering the separate state should have this care for the body which he is about to leave to the worms? Nay, he is a believer in Jesus as "the resurrection and the life;" this belief prompts his dying words; and it shall have to be said of him, as of Joseph, that "by faith" yea, "by faith," he "gave commandment concerning his bones."

GOD'S–ACRE.

H. W. Longfellow.

I like the ancient Saxon phrase, which calls
  The burial ground God's-Acre. It is just;
It consecrates each grave within its walls,
  And breathes a benison o'er the sleeping dust.

God's-Acre! Yes, that blesséd name imparts
  Comfort to those who in the grave have sown
The seed that they had garnered in their hearts,
  Their bread of life, alas! no more their own.

Into its furrows shall we all be cast,
  In the sure faith that we shall rise again
At the great harvest, when th' archangel's blast
  Shall winnow, like a fan, the chaff and grain.

Then shall the good stand in immortal bloom
  In the fair gardens of that second birth;
And each bright blossom mingle its perfume
  With that of flowers which never bloomed on earth.

With thy rude ploughshare, Death, turn up the sod,
And spread the furrow for the seed we sow;
This is the field and Acre of our God—
This is the place where human harvests grow.

THEY ARE ALL GONE.

HENRY VAUGHAN.

THEY are all gone into a world of light,
And I alone sit lingering here;
Their very memory is fair and bright,
And my sad thoughts doth clear.

It glows and glitters in my cloudy breast
Like stars upon some gloomy grove,
Or those faint beams in which the hill is dressed
After the sun's remove.

I see them walking in an air of glory,
Whose light doth trample on my days—
My days which are at best but dull and hoary,
Mere glimmerings and decays.

O, holy hope, and high humility—
High as the heavens above!
These are your walks, and ye have showed them me,
To kindle my cold love.

Dear, beauteous Death — the jewel of the just —
Shining nowhere but in the dark;
What mysteries do lie beyond thy dust,
Could man outlook that mark!

He that hath found some fledged bird's nest may know
At first sight if the bird be flown;
But what fair field or grove he sings in now,
That is to him unknown.

And yet as angels, in some brighter dreams,
Call to the soul, when man doth sleep,
So some strange thoughts transcend our wonted themes,
And into glory peep.

IN AFFLICTION LOOK TO JESUS.

OCTAVIUS WINSLOW.

In each season of affliction, to whom can we more appropriately look than to Jesus? He was preëminently the man of sorrows, and acquainted with grief. If you would tell your grief to one who knew grief as none ever knew it; if you would weep upon the bosom of one who wept as none ever wept; if you would disclose your sorrow to one who sorrowed as none ever sorrowed; if you would bare your wound to one who was wounded as none ever was wounded, —then, in your affliction, turn from all creature sympathy and succor, and *look to Jesus:* to a kinder nature, to a tenderer bosom, to a deeper love, to a more powerful arm, to a more sympathizing friend, you could not take your trial, your affliction, and your sorrow. He is prepared to imbosom himself in your deepest grief, and to make your circumstances all his own. So completely and personally is he one with you, that nothing can affect you that does not instantly touch him. . . . God's family is a sorrowing family. "I have chosen thee," he says, "in the furnace of affliction." "I will leave in the midst of thee a poor and an afflicted people." The history of the church finds its fittest emblem in the burning, yet unconsumed, bush which Moses saw. Man is "born to sorrow;" but the believer is "*appointed* thereunto." It would seem to be a condition inseparable from his high calling. If he is a "chosen vessel," it is in the "furnace of affliction." If he is an adopted child, "chastening" is the mark. If he is journeying to the heavenly kingdom, his path lies through "much tribulation." But if his sufferings abound, much more so do his consolations. To be comforted by God may well reconcile us to any sorrow with which it may please our heavenly Father to invest us. . . . Go and breathe your sorrows into God's heart, and he will comfort you. Blessed sorrow if, in the time of your bereavement, your grief, and your solitude, you are led to Jesus, making him your Savior, your Friend, your Counsellor, and your Shield. Blessed loss, if it be compensated by a knowledge of God, if you find in him a Father now, to whom you will transfer your ardent affections, upon whom you will repose your bleeding heart, and in whom you will trust.

BROKEN TIES.

HOME JOURNAL.

'Tis something very sad
To place our hand in Memory's, and retrace
With her the paths that trailing years have worn,
And, in green spots which she shall point us out,
Pause to recount who sat beside us there,
And listen while she tells us of the Hours
That trooped before us, hand in hand with Joy,
When we, too, joined the mirthful revellers,
And thought—if thought, indeed, would sometimes come—
Of life as all one sunbright holiday.
How vividly they seem to stand again—
Those dear companions of my morning time—
In the familiar places! How I hear
Their silvery laughter, like the chime of bells,
Ringing the harmonies of happy hearts!
The youth, with flushing cheek, and kindling eye,
And form and mien of manliest dignity;
The graceful girl, with brow most eloquent
Of love and beauty; pensive womanhood,

And buoyant, bright-haired children. Eagerly
I turn to clasp them, but they melt away,
And, phantom-like, all vanish; and I find
'Twas but a mirage memory had evoked,
To taunt my longing vision. Deeper, then,
And with an aching sense too real, comes
Back to my heart that saddest consciousness,
That *only* thus can I behold again
The sweet-remembered faces that are gone.

Mysteriously a dread and unseen hand
Cuts at a blow the thousand golden cords
Whose twisting Love had labored at for years.
And they who seemed a portion of ourselves —
Who sat with us beside the household hearth,
And at the cheerful board, — who had no joy
Or sorrow that we knew not of, — are snatched
Forever from our sight; and we are left,
Amid our blinding tears, to gather up
The shattered threads that were so powerless
To fasten down to earth the subtile soul.
They have no room for grief, regret, or pain;
Seraph capacity of thought is theirs,
And God and glory overwhelm it all.
The rupture and the agony are *ours*,
Who, in our human weakness, oft forget,
Or fail to follow, with an eye of faith,
The joyous spirit in its skyward flight;
But weep with an absorbing grief around
The empty cage of clay. Yet even *then*
Gleams forth, with iris beauty, through the storm,
This blessèd hope — that all these broken ties

Shall be rejoined again; that we shall meet,
And have the seal of immortality
Set to our love by God's own sovereign hand,
Who thus shall weave these golden, earthly threads
Into the garments that we wear above.

"Lord, make me to know mine end, and the measure of my days, what it is; that I may know how frail I am. Behold, thou hast made my days as a hand breadth, and mine age is as nothing before thee."—PSALM xxxix.

"Whatsoever thy hand findeth to do, do it with thy might; for there is no work, nor device, nor knowledge, nor wisdom, in the grave whither thou goest."—ECCLESIASTES ix.

CONSOLATION.

ELIZABETH BARRETT BROWNING.

ALL are not taken; there are left behind
Living belovéds, tender looks to bring,
And make the daylight still a blesséd thing,
And tender voices, to make soft the wind;
But if it were not so,—if I could find
No love in all the world to answer me,
Nor any pathway but rang hollowly,
Where "dust to dust" the love from life disjoined,—
And if with parchéd lips, as in a dearth
Of water springs the very deserts claim,
I uttered to those sepulchres unmoving
The bitter cry, "Where are ye, O my loving?"
I know a voice would sound, Daughter, I AM!
Can I suffice for HEAVEN, and not for *earth?*

CONSOLATORY EPISTLE.

St. Basil.

It is the command of God not to lament the dead, in the faith of Christ, because of the hope of the resurrection, and that there are great crowns laid up for great patience. If we suffer reason to sing these things in our ears, we may find some moderate end of this evil; and therefore I exhort thee, as a generous combatant, to fortify thyself against the heaviness of this stroke, and not lie down under the weight of sorrow. Being persuaded, that though the reason of God's dispensations are out of our reach, yet we ought entirely to accept that which is ordered by one so wise and loving, although it be heavy and grievous to be borne; for he knows how to appoint to every one what is profitable, and why he hath set unequal terms to our life. The cause is incomprehensible by us, why some are carried away sooner, and others tarry longer in this toilsome and miserable life; so that we ought, in all things, to adore his loving kindness, and not to take any thing ill at his hands, remembering the great and famous voice of Job, who, when he heard that his ten children were all struck dead in one moment, said, "The Lord gave, the Lord hath taken away: as it pleased the Lord, so it is come to pass." Let us make this admirable language our own. They are rewarded, with an equal recompense, by the just Judge, who perform the same worthy actions. We are not robbed of a friend, but only have restored him to the Lender; nor is his life extinct, but only translated to a better. The earth doth not cover our beloved, but heaven hath received him: let us tarry a while, and we shall be in his company.

"But the salvation of the righteous is of the Lord: he is their strength in the time of trouble. And the Lord shall help them; he shall deliver them from the wicked, and save them, because they trust in him." — PSALM xxxvii.

THE MUCH-LOVED DEAD.

MARY E. LEE.

"O LA vita! O la morte!
Belle e dolce morir, fee certo allora,
Che amante in vita, amato in morte."

TASSO.

THE dead! the much-loved dead!
Who doth not yearn to know
The secret of their dwelling-place,
And to what land they go?
What heart but asks, with ceaseless tone,
For some sure knowledge of *its own?*

We cannot blot them out
From memory's written page;

We cannot count them strangers; but,
  As birds in prison cage,
We beat against the iron bar
That keeps us from these friends afar.

Oblivion may not hang
  Its curtain o'er their grave;
There is no water we can sip,
  Like Lethe's lulling wave.
But fond affection's moaning wail
Breaks from us like the autumn gale.

Grief cannot win them back;
  And yet, with frequent tear,
We question of their hidden lot,
  And list, with throbbing ear,
For some low answer that may roll
Through the hushed temple of the soul.

We love them — love them yet!
  But is our love returned?
Is memory's hearth now cold and dark
  Where once the heart-fire burned?
Nor do the laborers now gone home
Look for the weary ones to come?

We wrong them by the thought.
  Affections cannot die:
Man is still man, where'er he goes —
  And O, how strong the tie
Which links us, as with fetters fast,
Unto the future and the past!

Death would be dark indeed,
  If, with this mortal shroud,
We threw off all the sympathies
  That in our being crowd,
And entered on the spirit land
A stranger, 'mid a stranger band.

Far pleasanter to think
  That each familiar face
Now gazes on us, as of old,
  From its mysterious place,
With love that neither death nor change
Hath power to sever or estrange.

O, who will dare to say,
  "This is an idle dream"?
Who, that hath given one captive dove
  To soar by its own stream,
But fancies that its breathings low
Float round them wheresoe'er they go?

Mother! couldst thou endure
  To think thyself forgot
By *her*, who was thy life, thy air,
  The sunbeam of thy lot?
Wouldst thou not live in doubt and fear,
If all thy bright hopes perished *here?*

And brother! sister! child!
  Ye all have loved the light
Of many a dearly-cherished one,
  Now taken from your sight;

And can *ye* deem that, when ye meet,
Hearts will not hold communion sweet?

Alas! if it be so,
  That in the burial urn
The soul must garner up the love
  That once did in it burn —
Better to know not of the worth
Of true affection on this earth;

Better to live alone,
  Unblessing and unblest,
Than thus to meet and mingle thought—
  Than from the immortal breast
Shut out the memory of the past,
Like daybeams from a forest vast.

O, no; it cannot be!
  Ye, the long lost of years,
'Mid all the changes of this life,
  Its thousand joys and fears,
We love to think that round ye move,
Making an atmosphere of *love*.

Ye are not *dead* to *us;*
  But as bright stars unseen,
We hold that ye are ever near,
  Though death intrudes between,
Like some thin cloud, that veils from sight
The countless spangles of the night.

Your influence is still felt
In many a varied hour ;
The dewy morn brings thoughts of you ;
Ye give the twilight power ;
And when the Sabbath sunshine rests
On your white tombs, ye fill our breasts.

No apathy hath struck
Its ice bolt through our hearts ;
Yours are among our household names ;
Your memory ne'er departs ;
And far, far sweeter are the flowers
Ye planted in our favored bowers.

"When thou passest through the waters, I will be with thee; and through the rivers, they shall not overflow thee: when thou walkest through the fire, thou shalt not be burned; neither shall the flame kindle upon thee." —ISAIAH xliii.

DAYS OF TRIBULATION.

KRUMMACHER.

EVEN the days of tribulation have their sweet and pleasing intervals, which they bring disguised under the gloomy mantle of sorrow, whilst other days present them to us openly and in festive attire; and although such seasons cause distress, yet they are like vernal storms, which open the springs and cause them to flow. They are the days in which the spices of the divine promises yield their perfume; and when a resurrection breath pervades the graves of the prophets of God, then these ancient and hoary comforters express themselves audibly to us, and their feet are beautiful upon the mountains. A number of passages, which in brighter days were either unheeded or unappreciated, burn now in our hemisphere, as blissful and wondrous luminaries. Openings and peaceful retreats are discovered in the temple of the Scriptures, of which we had previously no idea. The spirit celebrates blissful and paradisiacal festivities; and often while the soul is lying in profound sorrow, or the flesh writhing in the glowing crucible, the mind rejoices that the refiner is near.

THE SPIRIT'S LAND.

AUTHOR OF SELWIN.

O, BEAUTEOUS are the forms that stand
  Beyond death's dusky wave,
And beckon to the spirit's land,
  Across the narrow grave!

No damp is on the freed one's brow,
  No dimness in his eye;
The dews of heaven refresh him now,
  The fount of light is nigh.

The parent souls that o'er our bed
Oft poured the midnight prayer,
Now wonder where their cares are fled,
And calmly wait us there.

The dearer still — the close intwined
With bands of roseate hue;
We thought them fair ; but now we find
'Twas but their shade we knew.

'Tis sweet, when o'er the earth unfurled
Spring's verdant banners wave,
To think how fair yon upper world,
Which knows no wintry grave.

'Tis sweet, when tempests earth deform,
And whirlwinds sweep the sky,
To know a haven from the storm
When worlds themselves must die ;

To know that they in safety rest,
The tranquil barks of those
Who, soaring on life's billowy crest,
Attained to heaven's repose ;

To know that brethren fondly wait
Our mansion to prepare ;
That death but opes that mansion's gate,
And lo! our souls are there!

A DEATH BED.

J. ALDRICH.

HER sufferings ended with the day;
  Yet lived she at its close,
And breathed the long, long night away,
  In statue-like repose.

But when the sun, in all his state,
  Illumed the eastern skies,
She passed through Glory's morning gate,
  And walked in paradise!

DEPARTED FRIENDS.

REV. M. HENRY.

OUR friends who have left us—where are they? Not lost, not perished. We are sure that to them, to whom to live it was Christ, to die will be gain. Where are they? They are where they are perpetually and perfectly blessed in the immediate vision and enjoyment of God, within the veil; infinitely more happy where they are than where they were.

Where are they? Why, they are in the mansions of light and bliss, that are in our Father's house above, in the paradise of God, where they hunger no more, nor thirst any more. They are in the best company, employed in the best work, and enjoying a complete satisfaction. Where are they? Why, they are where there are no complaints; nothing to interrupt their communion with God, or cast a damp upon their spirits. Death has done that for them which ordinances could not do; has perfectly freed them from that body of sin and death which was here their constant burden, and hath set them forever out of the reach of temptation. The spirits of the just are there made perfect, beyond the perfection of Adam in innocency, for they are immutably confirmed in it. Where are they? Why, they are where they would be — in their centre, in their element. They are where they longed to be — in that blessed state, towards which, while they were here, they were still reaching forth and pressing forward.

THE DEPARTED.

Park Benjamin.

The departed! the departed!
  They visit us in dreams,
And they glide above our memories
  Like shadows over streams;

But where the cheerful lights of home
  In constant lustre burn,
The departed, the departed
  Can never more return!

The good, the brave, the beautiful,
  How dreamless is their sleep,
Where rolls the dirge-like music
  Of the ever-tossing deep!
Or where the surging night winds
  Pale winter's robes have spread
Above the narrow palaces,
  In the cities of the dead!

I look around, and feel the awe
  Of one who walks alone
Among the wrecks of former days,
  In mournful ruin strewn;
I start to hear the stirring sounds
  Among the cypress trees,
For the voice of the departed
  Is borne upon the breeze.

That solemn voice! it mingles with
  Each free and careless strain;
I scarce can think earth's minstrelsy
  Will cheer my heart again.
The melody of summer waves,
  The thrilling notes of birds,
Can never be so dear to me
  As their remembered words.

I sometimes dream their pleasant smiles
  Still on me sweetly fall,
Their tones of love I faintly hear
  My name in sadness call.
I *know* that they are happy,
  With their angel plumage on;
But my heart is very desolate
  To think that they are gone.

MEEKNESS UNDER THE CHASTENING ROD.

ARCHBISHOP LEIGHTON.

IN private, personal correctings, let us learn to behave ourselves meekly and humbly, as the children of so great and good a Father; whatsoever he inflicts, not to murmur, nor entertain a fretful thought of it. Besides the undutifulness and unseemliness of it, how vain is it! What gain we by struggling, and casting up our hand to cast off the rod, but the more lashes? Our only way is to kneel and fold under his hands, and kiss his rod, and, even while he is smiting us, to be blessing him, sending up confessions of his righteousness, and goodness, and faithfulness, only entreating for the turning away of his wrath, though it should be with the continuing of our affliction. That is here the style of the prophet's prayer — *Correct me, O Lord, but not in anger.* And according to this suit, even where troubles are chastisements for sin, yet a child of God may find much sweetness, reading much of God's love in so dealing with him, in not suffering him to grow wanton and forget him, as, in much ease, even his own children sometimes do. And as they may find much of God's love to them in sharp corrections, they may raise and act much of their love to him in often-repeated resignments and submissions of themselves, and ready consenting to, yea, rejoicing in, his good pleasure, even in those things which to their flesh and sense are most unpleasant.

ON THE DEATH OF EDWARD PAYSON, D. D.

N. P. WILLIS.

A SERVANT of the living God is dead!
His errand hath been well and early done,
And early hath he gone to his reward.
He shall come no more forth, but to his sleep
Hath silently lain down, and so shall rest.

Would you bewail our brother? He hath gone
To Abraham's bosom. He shall no more thirst,
Nor hunger, but forever in the eye,
Holy and meek, of Jesus, he may look,
Unchided, and untempted, and unstained.
Would ye bewail our brother? He hath gone
To sit down with the prophets by the clear
And crystal waters; he hath gone to list

Isaiah's harp and David's, and to walk
With Enoch, and Elijah, and the host
Of the just men made perfect. He shall bow
At Gabriel's hallelujah, and unfold
The scroll of the Apocalypse with John,
And talk of Christ with Mary, and go back
To the last supper, and the garden prayer
With the beloved disciple. He shall hear
The story of the Incarnation told
By Simeon, and the Triune mystery
Burning upon the fervent lips of Paul.
He shall have wings of glory, and shall soar
To the remoter firmaments, and read
The order and the harmony of stars;
And, in the might of knowledge, he shall bow
In the deep pauses of archangel harps,
And, humble as the seraphim, shall cry,
Who, by his searching, finds thee out, O God?

There shall he meet his children who have gone
Before him; and as other years roll on,
And his loved flock go up to him, his hand
Again shall lead them gently to the Lamb,
And bring them to the living waters there.

Is it so good to die? and shall we mourn
That he is taken early to his rest?
Tell me,— O mourner for the man of God,—
Shall we bewail our brother — that he died?

"As Christ's body, when it was in the grave, did there rest in hope, *so shall the bodies of the saints*, when they lay them down in the dust: 'My flesh, also, shall rest in hope,' saith Christ. (Ps. xvi. 9.) In like manner the saints commit their bodies to the dust in hope: 'The righteous hath hope in his death.' (Prov. xiv. 32.) And as Christ's hope was not a vain hope, so neither shall their hope be vain." — FLAVEL.

THE TOMB NOT FEARFUL TO THE CHRISTIAN.

HERVEY.

As the roots, even of our choicest flowers, when deposited in the ground, are rude and ungraceful, but when they spring up into blooming life are most elegant and splendid, so the flesh of a saint, when committed to the dust, alas! what is it? A heap of corruption, a mass of putrefying clay. But when it obeys the great archangel's call, and starts into a new existence, what an astonishing change ensues! What a most ennobling improvement takes place! That which is sown in *weakness* was raised in all the vivacity of *power*. That which was sown in *deformity* is raised in the bloom of celestial *beauty*. Exalted, refined, and glorified, it will shine "as the brightness of the firmament," when it darts the inimitable blue through the fleeces — the snowy fleeces — of some cleaving cloud. Fear not, then, thou faithful Christian; fear not, at the appointed time, to descend into the tomb. The *soul* thou mayst trust with thy omnipotent Redeemer, who is Lord of the unseen world, "who has the keys of hell and of death." Most safely mayst thou trust thy better part in those beneficent hands, which were pierced with nails, and fastened to the ignominious tree, for thy salvation. With regard to thy *earthly tabernacle*, be not dismayed. It is taken down only to be rebuilt upon a diviner plan, and in a more heavenly form. If it retires into the shadow of death, and lies immured in the gloom of the grave, it is only to return from a short confinement to endless liberty. If it falls into dissolution, it is in order to rise more illustrious from its ruins, and wear an infinitely brighter face of perfection and of glory.

FOOTSTEPS OF ANGELS.

LONGFELLOW.

WHEN the hours of day are numbered,
And the voices of the night
Wake the better soul, that slumbered,
To a holy, calm delight;

Ere the evening lamps are lighted,
And, like phantoms grim and tall,
Shadows from the fitful firelight
Dance upon the parlor wall;

Then the forms of the departed
Enter at the open door;

The belovéd, the true-hearted,
  Come to visit me once more.

He, the young and strong, who cherished
  Noble longings for the strife,
By the roadside fell and perished,
  Weary with the march of life.

They, the holy ones and weakly,
  Who the cross of suffering bore,
Folded their pale hands so meekly,
  Spake with us on earth no more.

And with them the being beauteous,
  Who unto my youth was given,
More than all things else, to love me,
  And is now a saint in heaven.

With a slow and noiseless footstep
  Comes that messenger divine,
Takes the vacant chair beside me,
  Lays her gentle hand in mine.

And she sits and gazes at me
  With those deep and tender eyes,
Like the stars so still and saint-like,
  Looking downward from the skies.

Uttered not, yet comprehended,
  Is the spirit's voiceless prayer,
Soft rebukes, in blessings ended,
  Breathing from her lips of air.

O, though oft depressed and lonely,
  All my fears are laid aside,
If I but remember only
  Such as these have lived and died.

TO A BEREAVED SISTER.

S. Wells Williams.

If it be not all of life to live here, and this life be rather a night than a life, as Paul calls it, then is your brother alive rather than dead. He has gone through the night, and now sees the day, the daystar, the sun, the temple, and holy city, which needeth no sun or moon — and we should rejoice. He has burst those goodly walls in which he was so stoutly ensconced, and is now at large in the plains and pastures, where the good Shepherd, leading his flock beside the still waters, gives them such aliment as we could not stomach; teaches them such mysteries as we could not fathom; rejoices them with such entertainments as would make us heady, and rewards them with Himself. I was greatly refreshed with your account of his sickness and death; for such testimonials cheer us onward through the days appointed to us. That you should mourn the departure of G—— is proper; for the sweet intercourse you had can be had no more; the mutual counsel and assistance can be no longer afforded; and all those grateful favors, which bind us so close to each other, are ended. Death is the worse in such cases for the living; and our loss seems the greater for the vividness with which memory retouches the incidents, places, and scenes connected with the departed. Thus the recital you have given of your brother's sickness has tinted the remembrance of the past months, spent so sunnily in your house in ——, with a brighter halo than before, because now I can hope, and do hope, to pass more joyous ones with him and you where sins and doubts cannot come.

TO MY BROTHER IN HEAVEN.

H. W. Rockwell.

I know thou art gone to the land of the blest;
  Thou art gone to heaven's beautiful shore,
Where the heavy laden of earth are at rest,
  And the wicked shall trouble no more.
Thou art gone to a land more lovely than this,
  By the footsteps of angel bands trod,
And the trials of life thou'st exchanged for the bliss
  That abides in the presence of God.

We have wept o'er the sod that grows green on thy tomb,
  Where Morning, with eyes full of tears,

Weeps her dew in the wild flowers, whose beautiful bloom
Seems most like the bloom of thy years.
A few days of sunshine, and then comes the blast
That fills the sad woods with its moan —
The bloom from the cheek and the blossom is past,
And the spirit forever is flown.

Thou art happy now. We would not call thee back
From thy home on that beautiful shore,
But patiently tread life's wearisome track,
Until life and its sorrows are o'er.
Then, this painful dream ended, we'll meet thee at last
In the beautiful land of the blest,
And forget all the trials and woes of the past
In the pleasures of infinite rest.

The soft winds shall sigh o'er thy dreamless sleep,
And the chirp of the merry bird,
At the shut of day, 'mid the twilight deep,
By the place of thy rest shall be heard.
Sweet odors that breathe from yon forests of pine,
Shall waft in the breeze from the glen ;
But the love that once woke in that bosom of thine
Shall ne'er be awakened again!

We could not call thee back! no; soft be thy sleep,
And green be the turf o'er thy head!
'Twere better by far for the living to weep,
Than to mourn o'er the lot of the dead.

Thou art happy and blest 'mid that holy band
  That look from heaven's beautiful shore.
Bear us, ye angels, to that sweet land,
  When life and its sorrows are o'er.

"Christianity teaches us to moderate our passions; to temper our affections towards all things below; to be thankful for the possession, and patient under loss, whenever He who gave shall see fit to take away." —Sir Wm. Temple.

BEREAVEMENT.

Elizabeth Barrett Browning.

When some belovéds, 'neath whose eyelids lay
  The sweet light of my childhood, one by one
  Did leave me dark before the natural sun,
And I astonied fell, and could not pray,
A thought within me to myself did say,
  "Is God less God that *thou* art mortal-sad?
  Rise, worship, bless him! in this sackcloth clad
As in that purple!"—But I answer, Nay!
  What child his filial heart in words conveys,
If him for very good his father choose
  To smite? What can he, but, with sobbing breath,
  Embrace th' unwilling hand which chasteneth?—
And *my* dear Father, thinking fit to bruise,
  Discerns in silent tears both prayer and praise.

"If you be afflicted, join prayer with your correction, and beg by it that God would join his spirit with it. Seek this in earnest, else you shall be not a whit the better, but shall still endure the smart, and not reap the fruit thereof. Rejoice in Him who fails not, who alters not. He is still the same in himself, and to the sense of the soul that is knit to him, is then sweetest when the world is bitterest. When other comforts are withdrawn, the loss of them brings this great gain, so much the more of God and his love imparted, to make all up. They that ever found this could almost wish for things that others are afraid of. If we knew how to improve them, his sharpest visits would be his sweetest: thou wouldst be glad to catch a kiss of his hand while he is beating thee, or pulling away something from thee that thou lovest, and bless him while he is doing so." — LEIGHTON.

THE EARLY DEAD.

WILLIS GAYLORD CLARK.

IF it be sad to mark the bowed with age
  Sink in the halls of the remorseless tomb,
Closing the changes of life's pilgrimage
  In the still darkness of its mouldering gloom,
O, what a shadow o'er the heart is flung,
When peals the requiem of the loved and young!

They to whose bosoms, like the dawn of spring
  To the unfolding bud and scented rose,
Comes the pure freshness age can never bring,
  And fills the spirit with a rich repose, —
How shall we lay them in their final rest?
How pile the clods upon their wasting breast?

Life openeth brightly to their ardent gaze;
  A glorious pomp sits on the gorgeous sky;
O'er the broad world Hope's smile incessant plays,
  And scenes of beauty win th' enchanted eye:

How sad to break the vision, and to fold
Each lifeless form in earth's embracing mould!

Yet this is life!—to mark, from day to day,
  Youth, in the freshness of its morning prime,
Pass like the anthem of a breeze away,
  Sinking in waves of death ere chilled by time,
Ere yet dark years on the warm cheek had shed
Autumnal mildew o'er the rose-like red.

And yet what mourner, though the pensive eye
  Be dimly thoughtful in its burning tears,
But should with rapture gaze upon the sky,
  Through whose far depths the spirit's wing careers?
There gleams eternal o'er their ways are flung,
Who fade from earth while yet their years are young.

IMPROVEMENT OF AFFLICTION.

REV. ROBERT HALL.

WE should be more anxious that our afflictions should benefit us than that they should be speedily removed from us; for they are intended to remove a far greater evil than any which they can occasion. It is, in reality, a most sparing and economical method which the divine Being employs, when he uses these, "our light afflictions," in order to remove our sins; for sin is the great disease of our nature, which must be removed if we are to be made happy. It is far better that this disease should be expelled by the use of means, however painful, then that, by the withholding of those means, it should be increased, inflamed, and cause our destruction. We must be partakers of his holiness, that we may be of his happiness; and if it is true that "tribulation worketh patience, and patience experience, and experience hope, and hope maketh not ashamed," then are our afflictions, duly received, to be numbered among our greatest blessings. This, then, is the light in which you should accustom yourselves to view your afflictions — as commissioned by God; as merited by your sins; as the effect of perfect parental care; and with an earnest desire to derive the benefit designed in your sanctification.

MY MOTHER'S GRAVE.

JAMES ALDRICH.

In beauty lingers on the hills
  The death smile of the dying day;
And twilight in my heart instils
  The softness of its rosy ray.
I watch the river's peaceful flow,
  Here, standing by my mother's grave,
And feel my dreams of glory go
  Like weeds upon its sluggish wave.

God gives us ministers of love,
  Which we regard not, being near:
Death takes them from us; then we feel
  That angels have been with us here.
As mother, sister, friend, or wife,
  They guide us, cheer us, soothe our pain,
And when the grave has closed between
  Our hearts and theirs, we love — in vain.

Would, MOTHER, thou couldst hear me tell
  How oft, amid my brief career,
For sins and follies loved too well,
  Hath fallen the free repentant tear;
And in the waywardness of youth,
  How better thoughts have given to me
Contempt for error, love for truth,
  'Mid sweet remembrances of thee.

The harvest of my youth is done,
  And manhood, come with all its cares,
Finds, garnered up within my heart,
  For every flower a thousand tares.
DEAR MOTHER, couldst thou know my thoughts,
  Whilst bending o'er this holy shrine,
The depth of feeling in my breast,
  Thou wouldst not blush to call me thine.

FRIEND AFTER FRIEND DEPARTS.

MONTGOMERY.

FRIEND after friend departs;
 Who hath not lost a friend?
There is no union here of hearts
 That finds not here an end:
Were this frail world our only rest,
Living or dying, none were blest.

Beyond the flight of time,
 Beyond this vale of death,
There surely is some blessėd clime
 Where life is not a breath,
Nor life's affections transient fire,
Whose sparks fly upward to expire.

There is a world above,
 Where parting is unknown —
A whole eternity of love,
 Formed for the good alone;
And faith beholds the dying here
Translated to that happier sphere.

Thus star by star declines,
 Till all are passed away, —

As morning high and higher shines
To pure and perfect day:
Nor sink those stars in empty night;
They hide themselves in heaven's own light.

BENEFIT OF AFFLICTION.

BAXTER.

AFFLICTIONS are God's most effectual means to keep us from losing our way to our heavenly rest. Without this hedge of thorns on the right hand and left, we should hardly keep the way to heaven. If there be but one gap open, how ready are we to find it, and turn out at it! When we grow wanton, or worldly, or proud, how much doth sickness, or other affliction, reduce us! Every Christian, as well as Luther, may call affliction one of the best schoolmasters, and, with David, may say, "Before I was afflicted, I went astray; but now have I kept thy word." Many thousand recovered sinners may cry, "O healthful sickness! O comfortable sorrows! O gainful losses! O enriching poverty! O blessed day that ever I was afflicted! Not only the "green pastures and still waters, but the rod and staff, they comfort us." Though the Word and Spirit do the main work, yet suffering so unbolts the door of the heart, that the word hath easier entrance. . . . It were well if mere love would prevail with us, and that we were rather drawn to heaven than driven. But, seeing our hearts are so bad that mercy will not do it, it is better to be put on with the sharpest scourge than loiter like the foolish virgins till the door is shut. O, what a difference is there betwixt our prayers in health and in sickness! betwixt our repentings in prosperity and adversity Alas! if we did not sometimes feel the spur, what a slow pace would most of us hold toward heaven! Since our vile natures require it, why should we be unwilling that God should do us good by sharp means? Judge, Christian, whether thou dost not go more watchfully and speedily in the way to heaven in thy sufferings than in thy more pleasant and prosperous state.

CONSOLATION SOUGHT AND FOUND.

J. Bowring.

When the clouds of desolation
  Gather o'er my naked head,
And my spirit's agitation
  Knows not where to turn or tread;
When life's gathering storms compel me
  To submit to wants and woes, —
Who shall teach me, who shall tell me,
  Where my heart may find repose?

  To the stars I fain would reach me;
There the God of light must dwell;

Sacred teachers, will ye teach me,
  Blessed instructors, will ye tell,
How my voice may reach that portal
  Where the seraphs crowd in throngs?
How the lispings of a mortal
  May be heard 'midst angel songs?

God and Father, thou didst give me
  Sorrow for my portion here;
But thy mercy will not leave me
  Helpless, struggling with despair;
For to thee, when sad and lonely,
  Unto thee, alone, I turn;
And to thee, my Father, only
  Look for comfort when I mourn;—

Nor in vain—for light is breaking
  'Midst the sorrows, 'midst the storms;
And methinks I see awaking
  Heavenly hopes and angel forms;
And my spirit waxes stronger,
  And my trembling heart is still,
And my bosom doubts no longer
  Thine inexplicable will.

"It is a great truth, wonderful as it is undeniable, that all our happiness—temporal, spiritual, and eternal—consists in one thing, namely, in resigning ourselves to God, and in leaving ourselves with him, to do with us and in us just as he pleases. When we arrive at this state of entire and unrestricted dependence on God's spirit and providences, we shall then fully realize that what we experience is just what we need, and that, if God is truly good, he could not do otherwise than he does. All that is wanting is, to leave ourselves faithfully in God's hands, submitting always and fully to all his operations, whether painful or otherwise."—MADAME GUYON.

I SEE THEE STILL.

CHARLES SPRAGUE.

I SEE thee still:
Remembrance, faithful to her trust,
Calls thee in beauty from the dust;
Thou comest in the morning light,
Thou'rt with me through the gloomy night,
In dreams I meet thee as of old:
Then thy soft arms my neck infold,
And thy sweet voice is in my ear.
In every scene to memory dear
I see thee still.

I see thee still
In every hallowed token round:
This little ring thy finger bound;
This lock of hair thy forehead shaded;
This silken chain by thee was braided;
These flowers, all withered now, like thee,
Sweet sister, thou didst cull for me;
This book was thine — here didst thou read;
This picture — ah, yes, here, indeed,
I see thee still.

I see thee still:
Here was thy summer noon's retreat;
Here was thy favorite fireside seat;

This was thy chamber—here, each day,
I sat and watched thy sad decay;
Here, on this bed, thou last didst lie;
Here, on this pillow, thou didst die.
Dark hour! once more its woes unfold—
As then I saw thee, pale and cold,
I see thee still.

I see thee still:
Thou art not in the grave confined—
Death cannot chain the immortal mind;
Let earth close o'er its sacred trust,
But goodness dies not in the dust.
Thee, O my sister! 'tis not thee
Beneath the coffin's lid I see;
Thou to a fairer land art gone;—
There, let me hope, my journey done,
To see thee still.

WORDS TO A MOURNING HUSBAND.

REV. ROBERT HALL.

You have learned, my dear friend, the terms on which all earthly unions are formed; the ties on earth are not perpetual, and must be dissolved; and every enjoyment but that which is spiritual, every life but that which is "hid with Christ in God," is of short duration. Nothing here is given with an ultimate view to enjoyment, but for the purpose of trial, to prove us, and "to know what is in our hearts; and if we are upright before God, to do us good in the latter end." You had, no doubt, often anticipated such an event as the inevitable removal of one from the other; and I hope neither of you were wanting in making a due improvement of the solemn reflection, and laying up cordial for such an hour. Still I am well aware that the actual entrance of death into the domestic circle is unutterably solemn, and places things in a different light from what we ever saw them in before. . . . This heavy blow is undoubtedly intended to quicken your preparation for a future world. It loudly says to you, and to all, "Be ye also ready; for in such an hour as ye think not, the Son of man cometh." God grant it may be eminently sanctified by weaning you more completely from this world, and "setting your affections" more entirely and habitually "on things that are above." You will then, in the midst of that deep regret such a loss has necessarily inspired, have cause to bless God that you were afflicted.

"Many are the afflictions of the righteous: but the Lord delivereth him out of them all." — PSALM xxxiv.

SHE SLEEPS THAT STILL AND PLACID SLEEP.

HERVEY.

She sleeps that still and placid sleep,
  For which the weary pant in vain ;
And, where the dews of evening weep,
  I may not weep again.
O, never more upon her grave
Shall I behold the wild flower wave !

They laid her where the sun and moon
  Look on her tomb with loving eye,
And I have heard the breeze of June
  Sweep o'er it, like a sigh.
And the wild river's wailing song
Grow dirge-like, as it stole along.

And I have dreamed, in many dreams,
  Of her who was a dream to me ;
And talked to her, by summer streams,
  In crowds, and on the sea,
Till in my soul she grew enshrined,
A young Egeria of the mind !

'Tis years ago — and other eyes
  Have flung their beauty o'er my youth ;

And I have hung on other sighs,
  And sounds that seemed like truth ;
And loved the music which they gave,
Like that which perished in the grave.

And I have left the cold and dead,
  To mingle with the living cold ;
There is a weight around my head ;
  My heart is growing old.
O for a refuge and a home
With thee, dead Ellen, in thy tomb!

Age sits upon my breast and brain,
  My spirit fades before its time ;
But they are all thine own again,
  Lost partner of their prime.
And thou art dearer in thy shroud
Than all the false and living crowd.

Rise, gentle vision of the hours,
  Which go like birds that come not back,
And fling thy pale and funeral flowers
  On Memory's wasted track!
O for the wings that made thee blest,
To "flee away, and be at rest."

KNOWLEDGE OF CHRISTIAN FRIENDS IN A FUTURE WORLD.

REV. JOHN M. MASON.

THE clay which we commit to the grave under that universal sentence, "Dust thou art, and unto dust shalt thou return," will be quickened again, and reassume, even after the slumber of ages, the organization, the lineaments, the expression, of that selfsame human being with whom we were conversant upon earth: otherwise it were a new creation, and not a resurrection; and will be reanimated by that selfsame spirit which forsook it at death: otherwise it were a different being altogether, and not the one with whom, under that form, we held sweet communion in this life, and walked to the house of God in company. It has, indeed, been questioned whether Christian friends shall know each other in the world of the risen. But why not? Did not the disciples know the Lord Jesus after his resurrection? Did they not know him at the moment of his ascension? Shall the body which he wore upon earth be the only one recognized in heaven? If Peter and Paul, if James and John, shall not be able to distinguish each other, upon what principle shall they be able to distinguish their Lord? And why should the body be raised at all, if the associations with which its reappearance is connected are to be broken and lost?

THE FUTURE LIFE.

WILLIAM CULLEN BRYANT.

How shall I know thee in the sphere that keeps
  The disembodied spirits of the dead,—
When all of thee that time could wither sleeps
  And perishes among the dust we tread?

For I shall feel the sting of ceaseless pain
  If there I meet thy gentle presence not,
Nor hear the voice I love, nor read again
  In thy serenest eyes the tender thought.

Will not thy own meek heart demand me there?
  That heart whose fondest throbs to me were given?
My name, on earth, was ever in thy prayer;
  Shall it be banished from thy tongue in heaven?

In meadows fanned by heaven's life-breathing wind,
  In the resplendence of that glorious sphere,
And larger movements of th' unfettered mind,
  Wilt thou forget the love that joined us here?

The love that lived through all the stormy past,
  And meekly with my harsher nature bore,
And deeper grew, and tenderer to the last,
  Shall it expire with life, and be no more?

A happier lot than mine, and larger light,
  Await thee there; for thou hast bowed thy will
In cheerful homage to the rule of right,
  And lovest all, and renderest good for ill.

For me the sordid cares in which I dwell
  Shrink and consume the heart, as heat the scroll;
And wrath hath left its scar — that fire of hell
  Has left its frightful scar upon my soul.

Yet, though thou wear'st the glory of the sky,
  Wilt thou not keep the same belovéd name? —
The same fair, thoughtful brow, and gentle eye,
  Lovelier in heaven's sweet climate, yet the same?

Shalt thou not teach me, in that calmer home,
  The wisdom that I learned so ill in this? —
The wisdom which is love — till I become
  Thy fit companion in that land of bliss?

I KNEW THAT WE MUST PART.

CHARLES SPRAGUE.

I KNEW that we must part — day after day,
I saw the dread destroyer win his way;
That hollow cough first rang the fatal knell,
As on my ear its prophet-warning fell;

Feeble and slow thy once light footstep grew,
Thy wasting cheek put on death's pallid hue,
Thy thin, hot hand to mine more weakly clung,
Each sweet "Good night" fell fainter from thy tongue ;
I knew that we must part — no power could save
Thy quiet goodness from an early grave ;
Those eyes so dull, though kind each glance they cast,
Looking a sister's fondness to the last ;
Thy lips so pale, that gently pressed my cheek,
Thy voice — alas ! thou couldst but try to speak ; —
All told thy doom ; I felt it at my heart ;
The shaft had struck — I knew that we must part.
  And we have parted, sister — thou art gone !
Gone in thine innocence, meek, suffering one.
Thy weary spirit breathed itself to sleep
So peacefully, it seemed a sin to weep,
In those fond watchers who around thee stood,
And felt, e'en then, that God, e'en then, was good.
Like stars that struggle through the clouds of night,
Thine eyes one moment caught a glorious light,
As if to thee, in that dread hour, 'twere given
To know on earth what faith believes of heaven ;
Then like tired breezes didst thou sink to rest,
Nor one, one pang the awful change confessed :
Death stole in softness o'er that lovely face,
And touched each feature with a new-born grace ;
On cheek and brow unearthly beauty lay,
And told that life's poor cares had passed away ;
In my last hour be Heaven so kind to me !
I ask no more than this — to die like thee.
  But we have parted, sister — thou art dead !
On its last resting-place I laid thy head,

Then by thy coffin side knelt down, and took
A brother's farewell kiss and farewell look;
Those marble lips no kindred kiss returned;
From those veiled orbs no glance responsive burned:
Ah, then I felt that thou hadst passed away,
That the sweet face I gazed on was but clay;
And then came Memory, with her busy throng
Of tender images, forgotten long;
Years hurried back, and as they swiftly rolled,
I saw thee, heard thee, as in days of old:
Sad and more sad each sacred feeling grew;
Manhood was moved, and Sorrow claimed her due;
Thick, thick and fast the burning teardrops started;
I turned away—and felt that we had parted.—
But not forever—in the silent tomb,
Where thou art laid, thy kindred shall find room;
A little while, a few short years of pain,
And one by one we'll come to thee again;
The kind old father shall seek out the place,
And rest with thee, the youngest of his race;
The dear, dear mother, bent with age and grief,
Shall lay her head by thine, in sweet relief;
Sister and brother, and that faithful friend,
True from the first, and tender to the end,—
All, all, in His good time, who placed us here,
To live, to love, to die, and disappear,
Shall come and make their quiet bed with thee,
Beneath the shadow of that spreading tree;
With thee to sleep through death's long, dreamless night,
With thee rise up and bless the morning light.

SANCTIFIED AFFLICTIONS.

FLAVEL.

SANCTIFIED afflictions are prescribed in heaven for purifying our corruptions: "By this, therefore, shall the iniquity of Jacob be purged; and this is all the fruit to take away his sin." (Is. xxvii. 9.) It is a glass to represent the evil of sin and the vanity of the creature, to imbitter the world, and draw thy affections from it. Fall in, therefore, with the gracious design of God; connect every affliction with prayer that God would follow it with his blessing. God kills thy comforts from no other design but to kill thy corruptions; wants are ordained to kill wantonness, poverty is appointed to kill pride, reproaches are permitted to destroy ambition. Happy is the man who understands, approves, and heartily concurs with the design of God in afflicting providences.

ON THE DEATH OF A SISTER.

ANONYMOUS.

Another of God's servants hath put on
The garment of salvation. Young, and loved,
And beautiful, as if this world of pain
Were not unangelled, she hath dashed aside
Earth's sweetest draught, and thirsting for the springs
Of a celestial fountain, hath gone up
To taste the coolness of the living stream.
Peace to thee, sister — peace. We weep that thou
Hast left us thus alone ; our fairest flower
Faded in spring-time beauty ; our first star
Gone out at eventide. With thy soft smile,
And the glad music of thy gentle voice,
And all the spells with which thou'dst garnered love,
Thou hast passed from us ; and in grief we tread
Life's desert pathway onward, sorrowing much
That thy beguiling ministry will cheer
Our weary steps no more. But O, for *thee*,
For thee, our sister, o'er a sinless heart
Folding a seraph's garment — to thy lip,
In the first thirst of an immortal thought,
Lifting an angel's chalice — who can weep ?
Joy, joy for *thee*, sweet sister ! Thou wilt feel
Life's bitterness no more. Thou hast put off
Earth's heavy raiment, and arrayed in white,

Hast gone to tread in holiness and joy
The house of many mansions. Joy for thee!
The gifted and the mighty of old time
Shall win thee from thy solitude, and teach
Thy lip the hallelujah to our God,
And all the hymns of heaven; and thou shalt rest
Under the branches of the tree of life,
And bathe thy fingers in the living stream
Whose waters have no murmur, and shalt win
A compass and a mastery of mind
To fathom the deep mysteries of God,
And thou shalt soar with Gabriel, and tread
The mighty chambers of the vaulted sky,
Spanning the universe as with a thought.
And such shall be thy labor; but thy depth
Of blessedness, whose fountain is the light
Of God's eternal presence, who can tell?
  Pray for us, sister, — if a spirit's lip
May breathe a prayer in heaven, — that we, from whom
Thou'st parted for a season, may so tread
This veil of sorrow, that when life hath passed,
We may go up to thee, and claim thy hand,
To lead us where the living waters flow.

"SORROW NOT, EVEN AS OTHERS WHICH HAVE NO HOPE."—1 Thess. iv. 13.

Rev. Charles Wesley.

If death my friend and me divide,
Thou dost not, Lord, my sorrow chide,
  Nor frown my tears to see;
Restrained from passionate excess,
Thou bidd'st me mourn, in calm distress,
  For them that rest in thee.

I feel a strong, immortal hope,
Which bears my mournful spirit up
  Beneath its mountain load:
Redeemed from death, and grief, and pain,
I soon shall find my friend again,
  Within the arms of God.

Pass the few fleeting moments more,
And death the blessing shall restore,
  Which death hath snatched away;
For me, thou wilt the summons send,
And give me back my parted friend,
  In that eternal day.

9*

FEAR OF DEATH.

JEREMY TAYLOR.

DEATH is a thing that is no great matter in itself, if we consider that we die daily, that it meets us in every accident, that every creature carries a dart along with it, and can kill us. And, therefore, when Lysimachus threatened Theodorus to kill him, he told him, that was no great matter to do, and he could do no more than the cantharides could; a little fly could do as much.

Of all the evils of the world which are reproached with an evil character, death is the most innocent of its accusation. For when it is present, it hurts nobody; and when it is absent, it is indeed troublesome, but the trouble is owing to our fears, not to the affrighting and mistaken object; and besides this, if it were an evil, it is so transient, that it passes like the instant or undiscerned portion of the present time; and either it is past, or it is not yet; for just when it is, no man hath reason to complain of so insensible, so sudden, so undiscerned a change. If we be afraid of death, it is but reasonable to use all spiritual arts to take off the apprehension of the evil: but therefore we ought to remove our fear, because fear gives to death wings, and spurs, and darts. Death hastens to a fearful man: if, therefore, you would make death harmless and slow, to throw off fear is the way to do it; and prayer is the way to do that. If thou wilt be fearless of death, endeavor to be in love with the felicities of saints and angels, and be once persuaded to believe that there is a condition of living better than this; that there are creatures more noble than we; that above there is a country better than ours; that the inhabitants know more and know better, and are in places of rest and desire; and first learn to value it, and then learn to purchase it, and death cannot be a formidable thing, which lets us into so much joy and so much felicity. "The dead that die in the Lord" shall converse with St. Paul, and all the college of the apostles, and all the saints and martyrs, with all the good men whose memory we preserve in honor, with excellent kings and holy bishops, and with the great Shepherd and Bishop of our souls, Jesus Christ, and with God himself. For "Christ died for us, that, whether we wake or sleep, we might live together with him." Then we shall be free from lust and envy, from fear and rage, from covetousness and sorrow, from tears and cowardice; and these, indeed, properly are the only evils that are contrary to felicity and wisdom. Then we shall see strange things, and know new propositions, and all things in another manner, and to higher purposes.

"Yea, though I walk through the valley of the shadow of death, I will fear no evil; for thou art with me; thy rod and thy staff they comfort me." —PSALM xxiii.

ON THE DEATH OF A FRIEND.

BISHOP HEBER.

THOU art gone to the grave! but we will not deplore thee;
Though sorrows and darkness encompass the tomb,
Thy Savior has passed through its portals before thee,
And the lamp of his love is thy guide through the gloom!

Thou art gone to the grave! we no longer behold thee,
Nor tread the rough paths of the world by thy side;
But the wide arms of Mercy are spread to infold thee,
And sinners may die, for the SINLESS has died!

Thou art gone to the grave! and, its mansion forsaking,
Perchance thy weak spirit in fear lingered long;
But the mild rays of paradise beamed on thy waking,
And the sound which thou heard'st was the seraphim's song!

Thou art gone to the grave! but we will not deplore thee,
Whose God was thy ransom, thy guardian and guide;
He gave thee, he took thee, and he will restore thee,
And death has no sting, for the Savior has died!

IN AFFLICTION DWELL UPON THE BREVITY OF LIFE.

REV. T. BROOKS.

To silence and quiet your souls under the afflicting hand of God, dwell much upon the brevity or shortness of man's life. This present life is not life, but a motion, a journey towards life. Man's life, saith one, is the shadow of smoke, yea, the dream of a shadow. Saith another, Man's life is so short, that Austin doubted whether to call it a dying life or a living death. Thou hast but a day to live, and perhaps thou mayst be now in the twelfth hour of that day; therefore hold out faith and patience, thy troubles and thy life will shortly end together; therefore hold thy peace, thy grave is going to be made, thy sun is near setting, death begins to call thee off the stage of this world, death stands at thy back, thou must shortly sail forth upon the ocean of eternity; though thou hast a great deal of work to do, a God to honor, a Christ to close with, a soul to save, a race to run, a crown to win, a hell to escape, a pardon to beg, a heaven to make sure, yet thou hast but a little time to do it in; thou hast one foot in the grave, thou art even going ashore on eternity; and wilt thou not cry out of thy afflictions? Wilt thou not mutter and murmur when thou art entering upon an unchangeable condition?

What extreme folly and madness is it for a man to mutter and murmur when he is just going out of prison, and his bolts and chains are just knocking off! Why, Christian, this is just thy case; therefore hold thy peace; thy life is but short, therefore thy troubles cannot be long; hold up, and hold out quietly and patiently a little longer, (Rom. viii. 18,) and heaven shall make amends for all.

DIRGE IN AUTUMN.

WILLIS GAYLORD CLARK.

'TIS an autumnal eve — the low winds sighing
To wet leaves, rustling as they hasten by;
The eddying gusts to tossing boughs replying,
And ebon darkness filling all the sky;
The moon, pale mistress, palled in solemn vapor;
The rack swift wandering through the void above,
As I, a mourner by my lonely taper,
Send back to faded hours the plaint of love.

Blossoms of peace, once in my pathway springing,
Where have your brightness and your splendor gone?
And thou, whose voice to me came sweet as singing,
What region holds thee, in the vast unknown?
What star far brighter than the rest contains thee,
Beloved, departed — empress of my heart?

What bond of full beatitude enchains thee
  In realms unveiled by pen or prophet's art?

Ah, loved and lost! in these autumnal hours,
  When fairy colors deck the painted tree,
When the vast woodlands seem a sea of flowers,
  O, then my soul, exulting, bounds to thee —
Springs as to clasp thee yet in this existence,
  Yet to behold thee at my lonely side;
But the fond vision melts at once to distance,
  And my sad heart gives echo — she has died!

Yes! when the morning of her years was brightest,
  That angel presence into dust went down;
While yet with rosy dreams her rest was lightest,
  Death, for the olive, wove the cypress crown:
Sleep which no waking knows o'ercame her bosom,
  O'ercame her large, bright, spiritual eyes;
Spared in her bower connubial one fair blossom —
  Then bore her spirit to the upper skies.

There let me meet her, when, life's struggles over,
  The pure in love and thought their faith renew, —
Where man's forgiving and redeeming Lover
  Spreads out his paradise to every view.
Let the dim autumn, with its leaves descending,
  Howl on the winter's verge! — yet spring will come:
So my freed soul, no more 'gainst fate contending,
  With all it loveth shall regain its home!

THOUGHTS AT THE GRAVE OF BELOVED ONES.

MRS. JULIA NORTON.

AGAIN has Autumn scattered over these precious mounds of earth her faded, leafy mantle. Lightly it rests upon their unobtrusive elevations, beneath which sleep some of earth's richest treasures.

And are these perishing mementoes all that remain of their deeply-cherished worth? No. The halo of glory with which their virtues have encircled their memory shall never fade away. Our heavenly Guide Book teaches us that "the memory of the just is blessed."

Then be still, my aching heart, and thankfully follow life's beaten path until we are permitted to meet again — to meet where their beatified spirits are bathing in immortal love and immortal knowledge. They have passed through the "chances and changes" of this mortal life, and plumed their wings for an everlasting flight, where they can calmly review life's stormy sea, and contemplate their future blessedness in their eternal home. They sought the path that leads up to the city of God, and thus entered into joy and felicity — into an eternity vast and shoreless. They have entered the swelling stream of bliss, which is mysterious and fathomless. Far beyond the troubled waters of time their ever-increasing capacity for enjoyment will perpetually rise, and fill to the brim their cup of felicity.

Imagination here droops her wearied pinions, yet still continues to wander in search of those beloved spirits which have soared to the invisible world, unwilling to break the chain that binds it to those so dearly loved, so fondly cherished. And although the wounded heart has passed through the hour when it bled at every ruptured tie, — when cares and heavy woes pressed long upon its very existence, until nought was left but meek submission, — the belief that it again will meet and recognize, in a higher and holier state of existence, those so dearly loved upon the earth, buoys up the heart, and bids it look forward to its initiation into the celestial world, where the long-incarcerated soul shall be free, and independent of the feeble inlets of knowledge by the senses. When the veil of mortality shall be riven, the stormy Jordan passed, and the world of abiding realities entered, — then the world of deceptive and fleeting shadows will have forever passed away.

Sweet is it to hold converse with the pious dead. A holy influence emanates from their blissful home, and fills the soul with a feeling of sacred and solemn awe. The spirit whispers peace, and fills the waiting caverns of the soul with the bright hope of again meeting those whom we believe to be in the abodes of redeemed and happy spirits. In vivid expectancy it awaits the morning of the resurrection, and the happy reunion of kindred souls, where no tear of grief bedews the cheek, no agonizing farewell rends the heart; where a purer and holier love will fill the bosom than earth has ever known; where dwell our kindred with the wise and good of untold ages; where the "open ear of the soul" will obtain knowledge from patriarchs and angels; where our immortal spirits shall go free, and, wafted by angel wings, survey the boundless ocean of eternity.

THE GRAVES OF A HOUSEHOLD.

MRS. HEMANS.

THEY grew in beauty, side by side,
  They filled one home with glee;
Their graves are severed, far and wide,
  By mount, and stream, and sea.

The same fond mother bent at night
  O'er each fair, sleeping brow;
She had each folded flower in sight—
  Where are those dreamers now?

One, 'midst the forest of the west,
  By a dark stream is laid;
The Indian knows his place of rest,
  Far in the cedar shade.

The sea, the blue, lone sea hath one —
He lies where pearls lie deep;
He was the loved of all, yet none
O'er his low bed may weep.

One sleeps where southern vines are dressed,
Above the noble slain:
He wrapped his colors round his breast
On a blood-red field of Spain.

And one — o'er *her* the myrtle showers
Its leaves, by soft winds fanned;
She faded 'midst Italian flowers —
The last of that bright band.

And parted thus they rest, who played
Beneath the same green tree,
Whose voices mingled as they prayed
Around one parent knee.

They that with smiles lit up the hall,
And cheered with song the hearth —
Alas for love, if *thou* wert all,
And nought beyond, O earth!

RETROSPECT.

M. F. Tupper.

How many years are fled!
How many friends are dead!
Alas! how fast
The past hath passed!
How speedily life hath sped!

Places that knew me of yore
Know me for theirs no more;
And sore at the change,
Quite strange I range
Where I was at home before.

Thoughts and things, each day,
Seem to be fading away;
Yet this is, I wot,
Their lot to be not
Continuing in one stay.

A mingled mesh it seems
Of facts and fancy's gleams;
I scarce have power,
From hour to hour,
To separate things from dreams.

Darkly, as in a glass,
Like a vain shadow they pass;
Their ways they wend
And tend to an end,
The goal of life, alas!

Alas? and wherefore so?
Be glad for this passing show;
The world and its lust
Back must to their dust
Before the soul can grow.

Expand, my willing mind,
Thy nobler life to find;
Thy childhood leave,
Nor grieve to bereave
Thine age of toys behind.

HEAVENWARD.

REV. A. C. COXE.

So, in our simple creed,
We drop this frail mortality we wear,
And—laud to Him who for our sakes did bleed,
And on his cross our bitter griefs did bear—
We know our ransomed nature certain heir
Of deathless being from its dying seed.

They who nurse hopes live every day an age,
And strive more fleet to live by living well:
And so we hasten on our pilgrimage,
Plucking earth's flowers, but fain in heaven to dwell.
Life, in our ear, doth mean eternity;
And Time, our staff, but speeds us on our way,
While all around poor voyagers we see,
Who bear it but to chronicle each day,
And notch the hurrying hours of destiny
In fearful units, numbering for dismay
The lavished seeds of immortality.
But O, our souls take no account of time,
For we are gazing into worlds sublime;
Our spirits are like song birds, nursed to light
In climates far too rude,
That, by a heavenly instinct, stretch their flight
To skies where such bright plumes were made to brood.
We know our kindred there,
In genial warmth, their golden plumage wear,
And sing their native notes forevermore:
We yearn for purer air,
And dream the music we were made to share,
As home we waft us from an alien shore.

THE PIOUS DEAD.

KRUMMACHER.

THE images of the pious dead continue to live in the hearts of their loving friends, like the image of the sun, which, reflecting itself in the waters, attracts them, at the same time, magnetically into its sphere ; and sorrow is transfigured in the ravishing prospect, "They went before us; we are following after." Yes, whatever the earth has borne or bears of what is truly great and glorious, though it may disappear from the corruptible eye, is nevertheless not lost to the children of God. It awaits us in the treasuries of heaven, in order to beam upon us there in superior splendor. Be patient, my friends ; time rolls rapidly away ; our longing has its end. The hour will strike, who knows how soon? — when the maternal lap of everlasting Love shall be opened to us; and the full peace of God breathe around us from the palmy summits of Eden.

RECOGNITION OF THE SAINTS IN HEAVEN.

DR. JOHN DICK.

It has been asked whether, in this blessed abode, the saints will know one another. One should think that the question was unnecessary, as the answer naturally presents itself to every man's mind; and it could only have occurred to some dreaming theologian, who, in his airy speculations, has soared far beyond the sphere of reason and common sense. Who can doubt whether the saints will know one another? What reason can be given why they should not? Would it be any part of their perfection to have all their former ideas obliterated, and to meet as strangers in another world? Would it give us a more favorable notion of the assembly in heaven, to suppose it to consist of a multitude of unknown individuals, who never hold communication with each other, or, by some inexplicable restraint, are prevented, amidst an intimate intercourse, from mutual discoveries? Or have they forgotten what they themselves were, so that they cannot reveal it to their associates? What would be gained by this ignorance no man can tell; but we can tell what would be lost by it. They would lose all the happiness of meeting again, on the peaceful shore, those from whom they were separated by the storms of life, of seeing, among the trophies of divine grace, many of whom they had despaired, and for whose sakes they had gone down with sorrow to the grave; of knowing the good which they had been honored to do, and being surrounded with those who had been saved by means of their prayers and labors. How could those whom he had been the means of converting, and building up in the holy faith, be to the minister of the gospel a crown of joy and rejoicing in the day of the Lord, if he did not recognize them when standing by his side? The saints will be free from the turbulence of passion, but innocent affections will remain; and could they spend eternal ages without asking, "Are our children here? Are our still dearer relations here? Have our friends, with whom we took sweet counsel together, found their way to this country, to which we travelled in company till death parted us?"

HEAVEN.

ANONYMOUS.

No sickness there,
No weary wasting of the frame away,
No fearful shrinking from the midnight air,
No dread of summer's bright and fervid ray!

No parted friends
O'er mournful recollections have to weep;
No bed of death enduring love attends,
To watch the coming of a pulseless sleep!

THE SPIRIT'S ECHO.

Mrs. Julia Norton.

An echo ! hush ! 'Tis from the spirit land !
How full the note ! and like to that loved band
That plumed their wings, and took their upward flight
When life was waning fast, and gloomy night
Sat brooding o'er my soul with visage dark ;
Then through the gloom they soared as doth the lark ;
Above earth's storms, high in the clear, blue sky,
And winged their way to blissful worlds on high.

The echo still ! Can it a message bear ?
Ye happy ones, escaped from earth's wild care,
Doth earthly love still waft your spirits o'er
The wave of time to this once cherished shore ?
Where, lingering near the hallowed, sacred spot,
There breathes a sigh for those whose weary lot
Marks still their path, amid life's storms and foam,
To that bright land, our promised happy home ?

Still, still the note ! How sweet, how low, how clear !
It breathes of love ; it murmurs ; list ! 'tis near.

ECHO.

" Where the waters of time and eternity meet,
Thou didst stand on the shore when dark sorrow beat

Sea-like, and dashing those whom she would wreck—
While the tears of thy heart bowed low thy frail neck.
Like a pure water lily, thou'lt rise from the storm;
Like a spirit inhaling the breath of the morn,
Like the eagle when soaring above his cloud nest,
Thou'lt be wafted on shore in the realm of the blest."

DETACHED THOUGHTS.

CECIL.

THOUGH we may endure much affliction, and pass through many deep waters, yet this is our honor and comfort, *the Lord is with us!* and then—what is difficulty?—what is tribulation?—what is death?—Death to a Christian is but an entrance into the city of God; it is but joining a more blessed company, and singing in a more exalted strain, than he can in this world.

What I do thou knowest not now; but thou shalt know hereafter—is the unwearied language of God, in his providence. He will have CREDIT every step. He will not assign reasons, because he will exercise faith.

LEIGHTON.

LET this be our way, when we cannot find ease among men, to seek it in God. He knows the language of his children, and will not mistake it; yea, where there may be somewhat weakness and distempers, he will bear with it. In all your distresses, in all your moanings, go to him, pour out your tears to him. Not only fire, but even water, where it wants a vent, will break upward. These tears drop not in our own lap, but they fall on his, and he hath a bottle to put them in; if ye empty them, there they shall return in wine of strong consolation.

Fenelon.

Thy will be done in earth, as it is in heaven. Nothing is done here, any more than in heaven, but by the will or permission of God; but men do not always love that will, because it is often opposite to their desires. If we sincerely loved this will of God, and only this, we should change our earth into a heaven. We should thank God for every thing, for evil as well as good, because evil would become good from his hand. We should not then murmur at the guidance of providence, but approve and adore it.

Molinos.

Be silent and believe. Hold thy peace, and let thyself be guided by the hand of God. Suffer in patience, and walk on in strong faith; and though it seems to thee, that thou dost nothing, and art idle, being so dumb and resigned, yet it is of infinite fruit.

JEAN PAUL RICHTER.

MAN has two minutes and a half to live—one to smile, one to sigh, and a half to love—for in the middle of this he dies! But the grave is not deep—it is the shining tread of an angel that seeks us. When the unknown hand throws the fatal dart at the end of man, then boweth he his head, and the dart only lifts the crown of thorns from his wounds.

BE one sorrow alone forgiven thee, or made good to thee—the sorrow for thy dead ones; for this sweet sorrow for the lost is itself but another form of consolation. When the heart is full of longing for them, it is but another mode of continuing to love them; and we shed tears as well when we think of their departure, as when we picture to ourselves our joyful reunion—and the tears, methinks, differ not.

H. BONAR.

HOW fast we learn in the day of sorrow! Scripture shines out in new effulgence; every verse seems to contain a sunbeam, every promise stands out in illuminated splendor; things hard to be understood become in a moment plain.

REV. THOMAS BROOKS.

SURELY these afflictions are but the Lord's pruning knives, by which he will bleed my sins and prune my heart, and make it more fruitful; they are but the Lord's potion, by which he will clear me, and rid me of those spiritual diseases and maladies which are most deadly and dangerous to my soul.

O. Winslow.

It is our wisdom to know that no pure, unmixed sorrow ever befalls the Christian sufferer. Our Lord Jesus flung the curse and the sin to such an infinite distance from the church, that could his faith but discern it, the believer would see nothing but love painting the darkest cloud that ever threw its shadow upon his spirit.

Anonymous.

One, on being asked how he bore affliction so well, answered, "It lightens the stroke to draw near to Him who handles the rod."

Sir Wm. Temple.

I know no duty in religion more generally agreed on, nor more justly required by God Almighty, than a perfect submission to his will in all things; nor do I think any disposition of mind can either please him more, or become us better, than that of being satisfied with all he gives, and contented with all he takes away. None, I am sure, can be of more honor to God, nor of more ease to ourselves. For, if we consider him as our Maker, we cannot contend with him; if as our Father, we ought not to distrust him; so that we may be confident, whatever he does is intended for good; and whatever happens that we interpret otherwise, yet we can get nothing by repining, nor save any thing by resisting.

ANONYMOUS.

WHY should we not speak of our pious, departed friends as having gone to heaven? Why should we not associate with their absence the bright glories of paradise, instead of the gloom of the grave? When a friend who resides at a distance from us has left us for his home, and has had a painful and perilous journey thither, when we know of his safe arrival among the objects of his affections, we do not, in our imaginations, dwell upon the perils of the way, but upon the joys he has reached.

DR. CHALMERS.

THERE may be audible music in heaven; but its chief delight will be in the music of principles in full and consenting harmony with the laws of eternal rectitude. There may be visions of loveliness there; but it will be the loveliness of virtue, as seen in God, and reflected back in family likeness from all his children.

SAURIN.

WHETHER God afflict us in love or strike us in wrath, whether he afflict us for instruction or chasten us for correction, our first duty under the rod is to acknowledge the equity of his hand.

KRUMMACHER.

AFFLICTION is a thorn, but still it is from God, and by it he pierces through the leaves of pride. Many trees grow better in the shade than in the sunshine. O, if God only be with us, then the furnace is changed into a fire of joy, a prison into a pleasure ground, an earthquake into a cheerful dance. Even the rod of his anger, like Aaron's rod, blossoms and bears almonds; or, like the staff of Jonathan, brings honey on its point.

GOD often lets his people reach the shore as on the planks of a shipwrecked vessel. He deprives us of the cisterns in order to make us drink out of the fountain of waters. He frequently takes away our supports, not that we may fall to the ground, but that he may himself become our rod and our staff.

IT is not one and the same to say, "God consoles me," and "God is my consolation." If the Lord console me, then my heart is light, clear, and cheerful, and into the sorrow of my soul flows the feeling of joy. Is God himself my consolation? then my heart may be torn, parched, and dark. I fear not, but am of good courage, and stand over my heart, and walk upon the waves, and am still. I have it not in feelings, but I have it in naked faith in that God who has sworn to be my God ; I have it in that faith which hath and possesses that which I neither see, nor taste, nor feel. Faith in Jesus is the grave of sorrow.

John Bunyan.

If thou canst hear, and bear the rod of affliction which God shalt lay upon thee, remember this lesson: thou art *beaten* that thou mayst be better. The Lord useth his *flail* of tribulation to separate the chaff from the wheat.

The school of the cross is the school of light ; it discovers the world's vanity, baseness, and wickedness, and lets us see more of God's mind. Out of dark affliction comes a spiritual light. In times of affliction we commonly meet with the sweetest experiences of the love of God.

Did we heartily renounce the pleasures of this world, we should be very little troubled for our afflictions ; that which renders an afflicted state so insupportable to many, is because they are too much addicted to the pleasures of this life, and so cannot endure that which makes a separation between them.

Young.

Death is the crown of life :
Were death denied, poor man would live in vain.
Death wounds to cure ; we fall, we rise, we reign ;

Spring from our fetters, fasten to the skies,
Where blooming Eden withers from our sight.
This king of terrors is the prince of peace.

MILLMAN.

It matters little at what hour of the day
The righteous fall asleep. Death cannot come
To him untimely who is fit to die;
The less of this cold world, the more of heaven:
The briefer life, the earlier immortality.

BROWNING.

God keeps a niche
In heaven to hold our idols! and albeit
He break them to our faces, and denied
That our close kisses should impair their white,
I know we shall behold them raised, complete,—
The dust shook from their beauty,—glorified
New Memnons singing in the great God-light.

WORDSWORTH.

Thou takest not away, O Death!
Thou strik'st—and absence perisheth,
Indifference is no more;
The future brightens on our sight;
For on the past hath fallen a light
That tempts us to adore.

SHEWELL.

AFFLICTIONS are the ministers of love,
By Heaven appointed:—happy if they serve
To bring us nearer home!—to wean our hearts
From toys and trifles; and to fix them there,
Where only lasting happiness is found!

RESIGNATION.

BISHOP KEN.

PERMIT me, Father, like thy dearest Son,
To cry, Not mine, but thy sole will be done;
Not mine,—for I am blind, and what to choose,
What to desire, I know not, or refuse:
I ill may good, and bitter sweet, may think;
Mistake my antidote, and poison drink.
But thine be done—for thou omniscient art
To know the wants and soundings of my heart.

FRIENDS, even in heaven, one happiness would miss,
Should they not know each other when in bliss.

MRS. HEMANS.

YE left me! and earth's flowers were dim
With records of the past;
And stars poured down another light
Than o'er my youth they cast:

Birds will not sing as once they sung,
  When ye were at my side,
And mournful tones are in the wind,
  Which I heard not till ye died!

SOUTHEY.

THEY sin who tell us love can die;
With life all other passions fly,
All others are but vanity.
In heaven ambition cannot dwell;
Nor avarice in the vaults of hell;
Earthly those passions of the earth,
They perish where they have their birth;
But love is indestructible.
Its holy flame forever burneth,
From heaven it came, to heaven returneth;
Too oft on earth a troubled guest,
At times deceived, at times oppressed,
It here is tried and purified,
Then hath in heaven its perfect rest.
It soweth here in toil and care,
But the harvest time of love is there.

CHILDREN IN HEAVEN.

ANONYMOUS.

WHO are they whose little feet,
  Pacing life's dark journey through,
Now have reached that heavenly seat
  They have ever kept in view?

. . . .

Each the welcome "Come" awaits,
  Conquerors over death and sin;
Lift your heads, ye golden gates,
  Let the little travellers in.

"While the child was yet alive, I fasted and wept: for I said, Who can tell *whether* God will be gracious to me, that the child may live? But now he is dead, wherefore should I fast? can I bring him back again? I shall go to him, but he shall not return to me." — 2 SAMUEL xii.

A COTTAGER'S LAMENT.

ANONYMOUS.

SWEET, laughing child — the cottage door
  Stands free and open now;
But, O, its sunshine gilds no more
  The gladness of thy brow.
Thy merry step hath passed away,
Thy laughing sport is hushed for aye.

Thy mother by the fireside sits,
  And listens for thy call;
And slowly, slowly as she knits,
  Her quiet tears down fall:
Her *little hindering thing* is gone,
And undisturbed she may work on.

THE REAPER AND THE FLOWERS.

H. W. Longfellow.

There is a Reaper whose name is Death,
  And, with his sickle keen,
He reaps the bearded grain at a breath,
  And the flowers that grow between.

"Shall I have nought that is fair?" saith he;
  "Have nought but the bearded grain?
Though the breath of these flowers is sweet to me,
  I will give them all back again."

He gazed at the flowers with tearful eyes,
  He kissed their drooping leaves;
It was for the Lord of Paradise
  He bound them in his sheaves.

"My Lord hath need of these flowerets gay,"
  The Reaper said, and smiled;
"Dear tokens of the earth are they,
  Where he was once a child.

"They shall all bloom in fields of light,
  Transplanted by my care;
And saints, upon their garments white,
  These sacred blossoms wear."

And the mother gave, in tears and pain,
  The flowers she most did love;
She knew she should find them all again
  In the fields of light above.

O, not in cruelty, not in wrath,
  The Reaper came that day;
'Twas an angel visited the green earth,
  And took the flowers away.

ON THE DEATH OF AN INFANT.

HERVEY.

YONDER white stone, emblem of the innocence it covers, informs the beholder of one who breathed out its tender soul almost in the instant of receiving it. There the peaceful infant, without so much as knowing what labor and vexation mean, "lies still, and is quiet: it sleeps, and is at rest." (Job iii. 13.) Staying only to wash away its native impurity in the laver of regeneration, it bade a speedy adieu to time and terrestrial things. What did the little hasty sojourner find so forbidding and disgustful in our upper world to occasion its precipitant exit? It is written, indeed, of its suffering Savior, that when he had tasted the vinegar mingled with gall, he would not drink, (Matt. xxvii. 34;) and did our new-come stranger begin to sip the cup of life, but, perceiving the bitterness, turn away its head, and refuse the draught? Was this the cause why the wary babe only opened its eyes, just looked on the light, and then withdrew into the more inviting regions of undisturbed repose?

Happy voyager! no sooner launched than arrived at the haven. . . . Highly-favored probationer! accepted without being exercised. It was thy peculiar privilege not to feel the slightest of those evils which oppress thy surviving kindred; which frequently fetch groans from the most manly fortitude, or most elevated faith. The arrows of calamity, barbed with anguish, are often fixed deep in our choicest comforts. The fiery darts of temptation, shot from the hand of hell, are always flying in showers around our integrity. To thee, sweet babe, both these distresses and dangers were alike unknown.

Consider this, ye mourning parents, and dry up your tears. Why should you lament that your little ones are crowned with victory before the sword was drawn, or the conflict begun? Perhaps the Supreme Disposer of events foresaw some inevitable snare of temptation forming, or some dreadful storm of adversity impending. And why should you be so dissatisfied with that kind precaution which housed your pleasant plant, and removed into shelter a tender flower, before the thunders roared, before the lightnings flew, before the tempest poured its rage? O, remember, they are not lost, but taken away from the evil to come. (Is. lvii. 1.)

DEATH OF THE FIRST BORN.

WILLIS GAYLORD CLARK.

YOUNG mother, he is gone!
His dimpled cheek no more will touch thy breast;
No more the music tone
Float from his lips, to thine all fondly pressed;
His smile and happy laugh are lost to thee:
Earth must his mother and his pillow be.

His was the morning hour,
And he hath passed in beauty from the day,
A bud, not yet a flower,
Torn, in its sweetness, from the parent spray;
The death wind swept him to his soft repose,
As frost in spring time blights the early rose.

Never on earth again
Will his rich accents charm thy listening ear,
Like some Æolian strain,
Breathing at eventide serene and clear;
His voice is choked in dust, and on his eyes
Th' unbroken seal of peace and silence lies.

And from thy yearning heart,
Whose inmost core was warm with love for him,

A gladness must depart,
And those kind eyes with many tears be dim;
While lovely memories, an unceasing train,
Will turn the raptures of the past to pain.

Yet, mourner, while the day
Rolls like the darkness of a funeral by,
And hope forbids one ray
To stream athwart the grief-discolored sky,
There breaks upon thy sorrow's evening gloom
A trembling lustre from beyond the tomb.

'Tis from the better land!
There, bathed in radiance that around them springs,
Thy loved one's wings expand;
As with the choiring cherubim he sings,
And all the glory of that God can see,
Who said, on earth, to children, "Come to me."

Mother, thy child is blessed:
And though his presence may be lost to thee,
And vacant leave thy breast,
And missed a sweet load from thy parent knee,
Though tones familiar from thine ear have passed,
Thou'lt meet thy first born with his Lord at last.

HYMN FOR AN INFANT'S FUNERAL.

REV. LEGH RICHMOND.

HARK! how the angels, as they fly,
Sing through the regions of the sky,
Bearing an infant in their arms,
Securely freed from sin's alarms.

"Welcome, dear babe, to Jesus' breast,
Forever there in joy to rest:
Welcome to Jesus' courts above,
To sing thy great Redeemer's love!

"We left the heavens, and flew to earth,
To watch thee at thy mortal birth:
Obedient to thy Savior's will,
We staid to love and guard thee still.

"We, thy protecting angels, came
To see thee blessed in Jesus' name;
When the baptismal seal was given,
To mark thee, child, an heir of heaven.

"When the resistless call of death
Bade thee resign thy infant breath,
When parents wept, and thou didst smile,
We were thy guardians all the while.

"Now, with the lightning's speed, we bear
The child committed to our care;
With anthems such as angels sing,
We fly to bear thee to our King."

Thus sweetly borne, he flies to rest;
We know 'tis well — nay, more, 'tis best.
When we our pilgrim's path have trod,
O, may we find him with our God!

AN ANGEL PRESENCE.

REV. R. C. WATERSTON.

It is noteworthy that children who are taken away by death always remain in the memory of parents as children. Other children grow old, but this one continues in youth. It looks as we last saw it in health. The imagination hears its sweet voice and light step; sees its silken hair and clear bright eyes, all just as they were. Ten and twenty years may go by; the child remains in the memory, as at first, a bright, happy child. . . . Its young and beautiful form moves before us: and what is such a memory but *an angel presence?* Certainly next to seeing an angel, is seeing with a parent's heart such a cherished form. Amidst this world of ambition and show, who shall say that this is not a means, under Providence, of subduing and spiritualizing the mind? . . . Thus, in order to cherish such a remembrance, we are at times willing to turn even from the charms of the living. The sigh becomes sweeter than the song. Sorrow subdued becomes a friend, and sacred joy is mingled with the tears of holy recollection. . . . Thus, as grief ascends the Mount of Time, she seems to pass through a state of transfiguration. The convulsive agony changes to passive sorrow, and querulous misgivings to quiet meditation. There must be distress; let, then, the gushing tears flow, for it is the course of nature; but, even with this, let there be the victory of the Christian faith, the glorious hope of our holy religion.

THOUGHTS WHILE MAKING THE GRAVE OF A NEW-BORN CHILD.

N. P. Willis.

Room, gentle flowers! my child would pass to heaven!
Ye looked not for her yet with your soft eyes,
O watchful ushers at Death's narrow door!
But lo! while you delay to let her forth,
Angels, beyond, stay for her! One long kiss
From lips all pale with agony, and tears
Wrung after anguish had dried up with fire
The eyes that wept them, were the cup of life
Held as a welcome to her. Weep, O mother!

But not that from this cup of bitterness
A cherub of the sky has turned away.

One look upon thy face ere thou depart!
My daughter! it is soon to let thee go!
My daughter! with thy birth has gushed a spring
I knew not of — filling my heart with tears,
And turning with strange tenderness to thee —
A love — O God! it seems so — that must flow
Far as thou fleest, and 'twixt heaven and me,
Henceforward, be a bright and yearning chain
Drawing me after thee! And so, farewell!
'Tis a harsh world, in which affection knows
No place to treasure up its loved and lost
But the foul grave! Thou who so late wast sleeping
Warm in the close fold of a mother's heart,
Scarce from her breast a single pulse receiving
But it was sent thee with some tender thought,
How can I leave thee — *here!* Alas for man!
The herb in its humility may fall,
And waste into the bright and genial air,
While we — by hands that ministered in life
Nothing but love to us — are thrust away,
The earth flung in upon our just cold bosoms,
And the warm sunshine trodden out forever!

Yet have I chosen for thy grave, my child,
A bank where I have lain in summer hours,
And thought how little it would seem like death
To sleep amid such loveliness. The brook,
Tripping with laughter down the rocky steps
That led up to thy bed, would still trip on,

Breaking the dead hush of the mourners gone;
The birds are never silent that build here,
Trying to sing down the more vocal waters:
The slope is beautiful with moss and flowers,
And far below, seen under arching leaves,
Glitters the warm sun on the village spire,
Pointing the living after thee. And this
Seems like a comfort; and, replacing now
The flowers that have made room for thee, I go
To whisper the same peace to her who lies
Robbed of her child and lonely. 'Tis the work
Of many a dark hour, and of many a prayer,
To bring the heart back from an infant gone.
Hope must give o'er, and busy fancy blot
The images from all the silent rooms,
And every sight and sound familiar to her
Undo its sweetest link; and so, at last,
The fountain — that, once struck, must flow forever —
Will hide and waste in silence. When the smile
Steals to her pallid lip again, and spring
Wakens the buds above thee, we will come,
And, standing by thy music-haunted grave,
Look on each other cheerfully, and say,
"*A child that we have loved is gone to heaven,*
And by this gate of flowers she passed away."

TO A MOTHER BEREFT OF AN INFANT DAUGHTER.

REV. HERMAN HOOKER.

God does nothing without a reason. That reason may have respect to you; it may have respect to your child; and not unlikely to both. He sees effects in their causes. Your case may have been this: you may have been in danger of loving the world too much, and he removed the cause in time. Her case may have been this: she may have been in danger from the growth of a corrupt nature, and he took her in the bud of being that she might grow without imperfection, "for of such is the kingdom of heaven." Think of your child, then, not as dead, but as living; not as a flower that is withered, but as one that is transplanted, and, touched by a divine hand, is blooming in richer colors and sweeter shades than those of earth, though to your eyes these last may have been beautiful, more beautiful than you will hope to see again.

WORDS OF LUTHER ON LOSING A DAUGHTER.

MICHELET'S LIFE OF LUTHER.

LUTHER, when he lost his daughter Magdalen, who died in 1542, said to his wife, who was bitterly weeping, "Dear Catharine, console thyself; think where our daughter is gone, for sure she has passed happily into peace. The flesh bleeds, doubtless, for such is its nature; but the spirit lives, and goes to the place of its wishes. Children do not dispute; what we tell them, they believe. With them all is simplicity and truth. They die without pain or grief, without struggling, without temptations assailing them, without bodily suffering, just as though they were merely going to sleep." Then, as he looked upon her, he said, "Dear child, thou wilt rise again; thou wilt shine like a star—ay, like the sun. . . . I am joyful in spirit, but O, how sad in the flesh! 'Tis marvellous I should know she is certainly at rest, that she is well, and yet that I should be so sad." On the same subject he writes thus to Jonas: "You will have heard of the new birth into the kingdom of Christ of my daughter Magdalen. Though my wife and I ought, in reality, to have no other feeling than one of profound gratitude for her happy escape from the power of the flesh, the world, the Turk, and the devil, yet the force of natural affection is so great, that we cannot support our loss without constant weeping and bitter sorrow — a thorough death of the heart, so to speak. We have ever before us her features, her words, her gestures, her every action in life, and on her death bed — my darling, my all-dutiful, all-obedient daughter! Even the death of Christ — and what are all other deaths in comparison with that? — cannot tear her from my thoughts, as it ought to do. . . . She was, as you well know, all gentleness, amiability, and tenderness."

DIRGE FOR A YOUNG GIRL.

James T. Fields.

Underneath the sod, low lying,
Dark and drear,
Sleepeth one who left, in dying,
Sorrow here.

Yes, they're ever bending o'er her
Eyes that weep;
Forms that to the cold grave bore her
Vigils keep.

When the summer moon is shining
Soft and fair,
Friends she loved in tears are twining
Chaplets there.

Rest in peace, thou gentle spirit,
Throned above ;
Souls like thine with God inherit
Life and love.

ACTIVE DUTY ALLEVIATES SORROW.

HANNAH MORE.

In my judgment, one of the best proofs that sorrow has had its right effect is, that it has not incapacitated for business ; *your* business being duties. Under the pressure of heavy affliction, it is soothing to the heart to sink down into the enjoyment of a kind of sad indulgence, and to make itself believe that this is right, as it is gratifying ; especially while it mixes some pious thoughts with this unprofitable tranquillity. But who can say, even after the severest loss, I have no duties, no cares in life, remaining? Much less can a tender mother say it, who has still so many looking to her advice, and, what is almost more, to her example. It is not the smallest part of the good that you may do them, to let them see what effect great trials have upon your mind, and that Christianity enables you to bear up against such a stroke. It is an excellent sign that, after the cares and labors of the day, you can return to your pious exercises and meditations with undiminished attention. This will be a good criterion by which to judge of your state.

A HYMN OF SORROW.

To the Memory of our little Freddy.

H. W. Rockwell.

"Into the silent land,—
Ah, who shall lead us thither?"

Into the silent land,
Thither, O thither
Didst thou go forth with none to comfort thee?
Didst thou no light in Death's dark country see?
No friend to lead thee by thy little hand,
Gently, gently
To the land
Of the dear departed,
Into the silent land?

Yes, yes; 'twas He who died,
Even Christ, the crucified;
'Twas he who bore thee gently to that shore,
Who stood beside thy pillow,
And led thee through the billow
And the agony and darkness,
Evermore,
As a father leads his child by the hand
To the land
Of the dear departed,
Into the silent land!

Thou art happy now at last,
This painful life o'erpast;
Thou'rt happy now at last, in heaven's unmeasured
regions.
Amid the shining band
Of God's pure and holy legions,
Like an angel thou dost stand,
And beckon with thy hand
From the land
Of the dear departed,
Beyond the silent land!

TO LITTLE FREDDY IN HEAVEN.

H. W. ROCKWELL.

SWEET spirit, from the earth untimely fled,
Dost thou come near me with thy silver wings?
Or is it some fair bird of heaven that sings
So sadly in my heart since thou art dead?
Alas! the hands that pillowed thy dear head,
The eyes that watched thee through long nights of pain,
Will nevermore behold thy face again;
For thou art gone unto thy narrow bed.
Yet if to broken hearts, that long have shed
Their bitter floods for thee in scalding rain,
Thou comest still, O, be it not in vain
That we, too, follow where thy feet have led,
Through this dark world to heaven's enchanted shore,
Where they who part on earth shall meet to part no more!

TO A BEREAVED FATHER.

ARCHBISHOP LEIGHTON.

It was a sharp stroke of a pen that told me your pretty Johnny was dead; and I felt it truly more than, to my remembrance, I did the death of any child in my lifetime. Sweet thing! and is he so quickly laid to sleep? Happy he! Though we shall have no more the pleasure of his lisping and laughing, he shall have no more the pain of crying, nor of being sick, nor of dying; and hath wholly escaped the trouble of schooling, and all other suffering of boys, and the riper and deeper griefs of riper years, this poor life being all along nothing but a linked chain of many sorrows and many deaths. Tell his mother she is now much more akin to the other world; and this will quickly be passed to us all. John is but gone an hour or two sooner to bed, as children use to do, and we are undressing to follow. And the more we put off the love of this present world, and all things superfluous, beforehand, we shall have the less to do when we lie down.

TO A BEREAVED MOTHER.

JOHN QUINCY ADAMS.

SURE, to the mansions of the blest
  When *infant* innocence ascends,
Some angel, brighter than the rest,
  The spotless spirit's flight attends.
On wings of ecstasy they rise,
  Beyond where worlds material roll ;
Till some fair sister of the skies
  Receives the unpolluted soul.

That inextinguishable beam,
  With dust united at our birth,
Sheds a more dim, discolored gleam
  The more it lingers upon earth.
Closed in this dark abode of clay,
  The stream of glory faintly burns ;
Not unobserved, the lucid ray
  To its own native fount returns.

But when the Lord of mortal breath
  Decrees his bounty to resume,
And points the silent shaft of death
  Which speeds an infant to the tomb,
No passion fierce, nor low desire,
  Has quenched the radiance of the flame ;

Back to its God the living fire
  Reverts, unclouded as it came.

Fond mourner, be that solace thine;
  Let Hope her healing charm impart,
And soothe, with melodies divine,
  The anguish of a mother's heart.
O, think! the darlings of thy love,
  Divested of this earthly clod,
Amid unnumbered saints above,
  Bask in the bosom of their God.

Of their short pilgrimage on earth
  Still tender images remain:
Still, still they bless thee for their birth,
  Still filial gratitude retain.
Each anxious care, each rending sigh,
  That wrung for them the parent's breast,
Dwells on remembrance in the sky,
  Amid the raptures of the blest.

O'er thee, with looks of love, they bend;
  For thee the Lord of life implore;
And oft from sainted bliss descend,
  Thy wounded quiet to restore.
Oft, in the stillness of the night,
  They smooth the pillow of thy bed;
Oft, till the morn's returning light,
  Still watchful hover o'er thy head.

Hark! in such strains as saints employ,
  They whisper to thy bosom peace;

Calm the perturbéd heart to joy,
  And bid the streaming sorrow cease.
Then dry, henceforth, the bitter tear ;
  Their part and thine inverted see :
Thou wert their guardian angel here,
  They guardian angels now to thee.

"God seldom gives his people so sweet a foretaste of their future rest as in their deep afflictions. He keeps his most precious cordials for the time of our greatest faintings and dangers. He gives them when he knows they are needed and will be valued, and when he is sure to be thanked for them, and that his people will be rejoiced by them." — BAXTER.

THE ENDURANCE OF AFFLICTIONS.

REV. ROBERT HALL.

LET none, when under affliction, think that they are under God's anger, so as to have lost his favor, and forfeited the complacency of their heavenly Father. We should, indeed, examine ourselves, to see if there be any reason for particular calamities, from our peculiar delinquencies in duty, or from corruptions which we have indulged ; and thus we should "turn unto Him that smiteth us." But we should consider our trials as springing from love, as having their origin in our imperfect state of character, as made necessary by our sins. We should consider that they are sent to subdue in us the inclinations of "the old man," and to form in us Jesus Christ, in all his features of "righteousness and true holiness." Thus the Christian regards afflictions no longer with that terror which they impress on a person not in a state of reconciliation with God, and who derives his view of events only from a general notion of the providence of God. To such persons they appear the beginning of evils, and they lead them to contemplate God more with terror and dismay than with confidence and delight. But the Christian under affliction considers that he is, indeed, under the rebuke of a heavenly Father, but that it is with a view to his benefit. He considers that God deals with him as with a son; that God is his Parent; that he measures every stroke; that he sits by the furnace and assuages the flame, or increases his strength to endure it; that he superintends the whole process; and that, if patience have its perfect work, he will come out of it benefited, and, as it were, purified from dross by the furnace. Those who live in prosperity, and wealth, and success, and who are strangers to trials, may boast of their pleasures and joys. But all this is a dark mark. They are, perhaps, abandoned of God, because they have rejected the various calls of his providence and Holy Spirit. A person, however benevolent, extends not his paternal care to strangers and foreigners, but he is most peculiarly attentive to his children; he takes pains with them; he will not allow them to contract evil habits, or to follow their corruptions, though, in correcting them, he do it at the expense of their present comfort. For all in our nature of discipline crosses our natural inclinations and wishes, and is attended with uneasiness and annoyance. To endure these afflictions and crosses, in some way or other, is an effect of necessity; but to endure them as a Christian is an act of grace. The Christian, convinced of the design of God in affliction, yields himself into his hands. He says, in humble prayer, "Correct me, but with judgment; not in thine anger, lest thou bring me to nothing." He recognizes the hand of God as afflicting; he looks beyond the instruments, the injustice or unkindness of men, the impressions of the wickedness of the worst of mankind. He sees the wicked as God's instruments. To have higher thoughts of God under his rebukes, to cherish an undiminished love of his character, to turn with penitence and resignation to the hand of him that smiteth; not to be like Israel, of whom the prophet says, "The people turneth not unto him that smiteth them, neither do they seek the Lord of hosts," is the genuine mark of filial grace. The child, when chastened by a parent, clings only the closer to that parent. Thus the Christian cleaves and clings closer, as it were, to his heavenly Father under chastisement. He does not run away to the paths of disobedience, and flee to a distance from God; but he approaches nearer to him, and inquires the more earnestly how to please him. This is to endure chastisement like a child, to vindicate the character of God, to understand the motives of his conduct, to advance in all things the designs of his grace.

DEATH OF AN INFANT.

MRS. SIGOURNEY.

DEATH found strange beauty on that polished brow,
And dashed it out. There was a tint of rose
On cheek and lip. He touched the veins with ice,
And the rose faded.
Forth from those blue eyes
There spake a wishful tenderness, a doubt
Whether to grieve or sleep, which innocence
Alone may wear. With ruthless haste he bound
The silken fringes of those curtaining lids
Forever.
There had been a murmuring sound,
With which the babe would claim its mother's ear,
Charming her even to tears. The spoiler set
The seal of silence.
But there beamed a smile,
So fixed, so holy, from that cherub brow,
Death gazed, and left it there. He dared not steal
The signet ring of Heaven.

MY CHILD.

REV. JOHN PIERPONT.

I CANNOT make him dead.
His fair, sunshiny head
Is ever bounding round my study chair;
Yet, when my eyes, now dim
With tears, I turn to him,
The vision vanishes — he is not there!

I walk my parlor floor,
And through the open door
I hear a footfall on the chamber stair;
I'm stepping towards the hall
To give the boy a call;
And then bethink me that — he is not there.

I thread the crowded street;
A satchelled lad I meet,
With the same beaming eyes and colored hair,
And, as he's running by,
Follow him with my eye,
Scarcely believing that — he is not there.

I know his face is hid
Under the coffin lid;

Closed are his eyes ; cold is his forehead ;
　　My hand that marble felt ;
　　O'er it in prayer I knelt ;
Yet my heart whispers that — he is not there.

　　I cannot *make* him dead.
　　When passing by the bed,
So long watched over with parental care,
　　My spirit and my eye
　　Seek it inquiringly,
Before the thought comes that — he is not there.

　　When, at the cool, gray break
　　Of day, from sleep I wake,
With my first breathing of the morning air
　　My soul goes up with joy
　　To Him who gave my boy ;
Then comes the sad thought that — he is not there.

　　When at the day's calm close,
　　Before we seek repose,
I'm with his mother, offering up our prayer,
　　Whate'er I may be *saying*,
　　I am, in spirit, praying
For our boy's spirit, though — he is not there.

　　Not there ! — where, then, is he ?
　　The form I used to see
Was but the *raiment* that he used to wear.
　　The grave, that now doth press
　　Upon that cast-off dress,
Is but his wardrobe locked : *he* is not there.

He lives; in all the past
He lives; nor, to the last,
Of seeing him again will I despair;
In dreams I see him now;
And, on his angel brow,
I see it written, "Thou shalt see me *there*."

Yes, we all live to God!
FATHER, thy chastening rod
So help us, thine afflicted ones, to bear,
That, in the spirit land,
Meeting at thy right hand,
'Twill be our heaven to find that—he is *there*.

SONGS IN THE NIGHT OF BEREAVEMENT.

OCTAVIUS WINSLOW.

AH, heavy as that night is, there is a song even for it, smitten, weeping soul. Jesus was bereaved. Can you not sing of this? "Jesus wept." Is there no melody in these words? O, yes! As one who himself knew and felt the blank which death creates in human friendship, as one whose tears once fell upon the cold clay, while no hand was outstretched to wipe them, he sympathizes with your present sorrow, and is prepared to make it all his own. Wide as is the chasm, deep as is the void, mournful as is the blank which death has created, Christ can fill it; and filling it with his love, with his presence, with himself, how sweet will be your song in the night of your sorrow!—"He hath done all things well." O, there is not a single hour of the long night of our woe, but if we turn and rest in Jesus, we shall find material for a hymn of praise such as seraphs cannot sing.

Nor must we pass by David's sweet song in the dark night of his domestic calamity and grief: "Although my house be not so with God, yet he hath made with me an everlasting covenant, ordered in all things and sure; for this is all my salvation, and all my desire, although he maketh it not to grow." (2 Sam. xxiii. 5.) The everlasting covenant which God has made with Jesus, and through Jesus with all his beloved people, individually, is a strong ground of consolation amidst the tremblings of human hope, the fluctuations of creature things, and the instability of all that earth calls good. . . . What a friend, what a brother, what a helper is Jesus! Never, no, never does he leave his suffering one to travel the night of bereavement unvisited, unsoothed by his presence. He is with you now, and of his faithfulness that never falters, of his love that never changes, of his tenderness that never lessens, of his patience that never wearies, of his grace that never decays, of his watchfulness that never slumbers, you may sing in the storm night of your grief.

THE DYING INFANT TO ITS MOTHER.

REV. R. CECIL.

"Let me go, for the day breaketh." — GENESIS xxxii. 36.

CEASE here longer to detain me,
  Kindest mother, drowned in woe;
Now thy kind caresses pain me;
  Morn advances — let me go.

See yon orient streak appearing,
  Harbinger of endless day;
Hark! a voice, the darkness cheering,
  Calls my new-born soul away!

Lately launched, a trembling stranger,
  On this world's wide, boisterous flood,
Pierced with sorrows, tossed with danger,
  Gladly I return to God.

Now my cries shall cease to grieve thee,
  Now my trembling heart find rest;
Kinder arms than thine receive me,
  Softer pillow than thy breast.

Weep not o'er these eyes that languish,
  Upward turning towards their home;

Raptured they'll forget all anguish,
While they wait to see thee come.

There, my mother, pleasures centre;
Weeping, parting, care, or woe
Ne'er our Father's house shall enter:
Morn advances — let me go.

As through this calm and holy dawn
Silent glides my parting breath,
To an EVERLASTING MORNING,
Gently close my eyes in death.

Blessings endless, richest blessings,
Pour their streams upon thy heart;
Though no language yet possessing
Breathes my spirit ere we part.

Yet to leave thee sorrowing rends me:
Now again this voice I hear:
Rise! — may every grace attend thee,
Rise, and seek to meet me there!

"In afflictions, we experience not so much what our strength is, as what is the strength of God in us, and what the aid of divine grace is, which often bears us up under them to a surprising degree, and makes us joyful by a happy exit; so that we shall be able to say, *My God, my Strength, and my Deliverer.*" — LEIGHTON.

LETTER OF CONDOLENCE.*

EDWARD PAYSON, D. D.

My dear brother and sister in Christ, and now brother and sister in affliction, the letters which accompany this will inform you why I write. I see and share in the poignant grief which those letters occasion; nor would I rudely interrupt it. I will sit down and weep with you in silence for a while; and when the first gush of wounded affection is past, when the tribute which nature demands, and which religion does not forbid, has been paid to the memory of your dear departed babe, I will attempt to whisper a word of consolation. May the "God of all consolation" make it such. Were I writing to parents who know nothing of religion, I should indeed despair of affording you any consolation. My task would be difficult indeed, nor should I know what to say. I could only tell them of a God whom they had never known, of a Savior with whom they had formed no acquaintance, of a Comforter whose consoling power they had never experienced, of a Bible from whose rich treasures they had never been taught to derive support. But in writing to you, my only difficulty is of a very different

* This letter was addressed by Dr. Payson, to two of his flock, who, in their absence from home, received with it the afflicting intelligence of the death of their only child.

kind. It consists in selecting from the innumerable topics of consolation contained in the Scriptures those which are best adapted to your peculiar situation. So numerous are they, that I know not which to mention or which to omit. May God guide my choice and direct my pen. It is needless, in writing to Christian parents, to *you*, to enlarge on the common topics of consolation. I need not tell you *who* has done this — who it is that gives and takes away.

I need not tell you, that "whom the Lord loveth he chasteneth, and scourgeth every son whom he receiveth." I need not tell you of the great duties of resignation and submission, for you have long been learning them in a painful but salutary school. And need I tell you that He who inflicts your sufferings knows their number and weight, knows all the pain you feel, and sympathizes with you, even as you once sympathized with your dear babe? for "as a father pitieth his children, so the Lord pitieth them that fear him." O, think of this: the pity, the parental pity, of a God! Who would not willingly be afflicted, to be thus pitied? Go, then, my dear brother and sister, and lean with sweet, confiding love upon the bosom of this pitying, sympathizing Friend: there deposit all your sorrows, and hear him saying, The cup which I give you, my children, will you not drink it? Remember, he knows all its bitterness. He himself mentions the grief of parents mourning for a first-born and only child as exceedingly great. Remember, too, that taking this bitter cup with cheerfulness from your Father's hand will be considered by him as an unequivocal token of your filial affection. "Now I know that thou lovest me," said he to Abraham, "seeing thou hast not withheld thy son, thine only son, from me." It requires the same kind of grace, if not the same degree of grace, to resign a child willingly to God, as to sacrifice it on the altar; and if you are enabled thus to resign your babe, God will say to you, Now I know that ye love me, seeing ye withheld not your child, your *only* child, from me.

If, at times when "all the parent rises in your bosoms," these consolations should prove insufficient to quiet your sorrows, think on what is the situation and employment of your dear departed child. She is, doubtless, praising God; and, next to the gift of Christ, she probably praises him for giving her parents who prayed for her, and dedicated her to God. She now knows all that you did for her, and loves and thanks you for it, and will love and thank you forever; for though natural ties are dissolved by death, yet those spiritual ties which unite you and your child will last long as eternity. She has performed all the work, and done all the good, for which she was sent to us, and thus fulfilled the end of her earthly existence; and if you have been the means of bringing into being a little immortal, who had just lighted on these shores, and then took her flight to heaven, you have reason to be thankful; for it is an honor and a favor. Neither your existence nor your union has been in vain, since you have been the instruments of adding one more blessed voice to the choirs above.

TO A MOTHER ON THE DEATH OF A DAUGHTER.

MRS. DANA.

MOTHER, I've news for thee from heaven ;
  Thy daughter boweth near the throne ;
O, canst thou not for her rejoice,
  Though thou art left alone?

Hast thou not seen her lovely eye
  Gaze on thee through her glittering tears,
Though thou didst strive from every ill
  To shield her tender years?

Mother, thy daughter weeps no more ;
  For all her tears are wiped away ;
Exhaled like dewdrops from the rose
  Beneath the sun's bright ray.

Mother, thy daughter is in *heaven ;*
  And pain can never reach her there ;
No sickness comes to those who breathe
  That pure, delightful air.

Look up with Faith's observant eye,
  And see thine ANGEL daughter now ;
I would not wish to call her back
  To this dark world — wouldst thou?

"O, no, O, no," I hear thee say;
"My SAVIOR hath his promise kept;
He comforts me;—and yet I must
Weep on,—for Jesus wept."

A CHERUB.

BISHOP DOANE.

"DEAR SIR: I am in some little disorder by reason of the death of a little child of mine, a boy that lately made us very glad; but now he rejoices in his little orbe, while we thinke, and sigh, and long to be as safe as he is."—JEREMY TAYLOR TO EVELYN, 1656.

BEAUTIFUL thing, with thine eye of light,
And thy brow of cloudless beauty bright,
Gazing for aye on the sapphire throne
Of HIM who dwelleth in light alone,
Art thou hasting now on that golden wing,
With the burning seraph choir to sing?
Or stooping to earth, in thy gentleness,
Our darkling path to cheer and bless?

Beautiful thing! thou art come in love,
With gentle gales from the world above,
Breathing of pureness, breathing of bliss,
Bearing our spirits away from this
To the better thoughts, to the brighter skies,
Where heaven's eternal sunshine lies,

Winning our hearts by a blesséd guile,
With that infant look and angel smile.

Beautiful thing! thou art come in joy,
With the look, with the voice, of our darling boy;
Him that was torn from the bleeding hearts
He had twined about with his infant arts,
To dwell from sin and sorrow far,
In the golden orb of his little star.
Here he rejoiceth in light, while we
Long to be happy and safe as he.

Beautiful thing! thou art come in peace,
Bidding our doubts and our fears to cease,
Wiping the tears which unbidden start
From the bitter fount in the broken heart,
Cheering us still on our lonely way,
Lest our hearts should faint or our feet should stray,
Till risen with Christ we at last shall be,
Beautiful thing, with our boy and thee!

HOPE.

BISHOP HEBER.

REFLECTED on the lake I love
To see the stars of evening glow,
So tranquil in the heaven above,
So restless in the wave below.

Thus heavenly hope is all serene ;
 But earthly hope, how bright soe'er,
Still flutters o'er the changing scene
 As false, as fleeting, as 'tis fair.

IN AFFLICTIONS LOOK TO THE SAVIOR.

FLAVEL.

In all the troubles and afflictions that befall you, eye Jesus Christ. Afflictions rise not out of the dust, nor do they befall you casually ; but he raises them up, and gives them their commission : "Behold, I create evil, and devise a device against you." (Jer. xviii. 11.) He selects the instrument of your trouble ; he makes the rod as afflictive as he pleaseth ; he orders the continuance and end of your troubles ; and they will not cease to be afflictive to you till Christ say, Leave off ; it is enough. His wisdom shines out many ways in them. It is evident in choosing such kinds of trouble for you as are best adapted to purge out the corruption that predominates in you ; in the degree of your troubles, suffering them to work to such a height as to reach their end, but no higher, lest they overwhelm you. O, think, If the devil had the mixing of my cup, how much more bitter would he make it! There would not be one drop of mercy in it ; but here is much mercy mixed with my troubles. There is mercy in this, that it is no worse. Am I afflicted ? It is of the

Lord's mercy I am not consumed, (Lam. iii. 22 ;) it might have been hell instead of this chastisement. There is mercy in his supports under it ; I might have been left, as others have been, to sink and perish under my burdens. Mercy in deliverance out of it ; this might have been everlasting darkness, that should never have had a morning. O the tenderness of Christ to his afflicted !

A MOTHER'S LAMENT,

ON THE DEATH OF HER INFANT DAUGHTER.

MONTGOMERY.

I LOVED thee, daughter of my heart ;
  My child, I loved thee dearly ;
And though we only met to part,
  How sweetly ! how severely !
Nor life nor death can sever
My soul from thine forever.

Thy days, my little one, were few ;
  An angel's morning visit,
That came and vanished with the dew ;
  'Twas here, 'tis gone—where is it ?
Yet didst thou leave behind thee
A clew for love to find thee.

The eye, the lip, the cheek, the brow,
  The hands stretched forth in gladness,
All life, joy, rapture, beauty now,
  Then dashed with infant sadness;
Till, brightening by transition,
Returned the fairy vision.

Where are they now — those smiles, those tears,
  Thy mother's darling treasure?
She sees them still, and still she hears
  Thy tones of pain or pleasure,
To her quick pulse revealing
Unutterable feeling.

Hushed in a moment on her breast,
  Life at the wellspring drinking;
Then cradled on her lap to rest,
  In rosy slumber sinking:
Thy dreams — no thought can guess them;
And mine — no tongue express them.

For then this waking eye could see,
  In many a vain vagary,
The things that never were to be,
  Imaginations airy,
Fond hopes that mothers cherish,
Like stillborn babes to perish.

Mine perished on thy early bier;
  No — changed to forms more glorious,
They flourish in a higher sphere,
  O'er time and death victorious;

Yet would these arms have chained thee,
And long from heaven detained thee.

Sarah, my last, my youngest love,
  The crown of every other,
Though thou art born in heaven above,
  I am thine only mother;
Nor will affection let me
Believe thou canst forget me.

Then — thou in heaven and I on earth —
  May this one hope delight us,
That thou wilt hail my second birth,
  When death shall reunite us,
Where worlds no more can sever
Parent and child forever.

SUBMISSION TO GOD IN THE HOUR OF TRIBULATION.

THOMAS A KEMPIS.

POSSESS thy soul in patience, and comfort will arrive in its proper season. Wait for me; and, if I come not, wait; for I will at length come, and "will not tarry." That which afflicts thee is a trial for thy good; and that which terrifies thee is a false and groundless fear. . . . "Let not thy heart be troubled, neither let it be afraid." "Believe in me," whose redeeming power has "overcome the world," and place all thy confidence in my mercy. I am often nearest thee when thou thinkest me at the greatest distance; and when thou hast given up all as lost in darkness, the light of peace is ready to break upon thee. All is not lost when thy situation happens to be contrary to thy own narrow and selfish judgment. It is injurious to thy peace to determine what will be thy future condition by arguing from present perceptions, and it is sinful to suffer thy spirit to be so overwhelmed by trouble, as if all hope of emerging from it was utterly taken away. Think not thyself condemned to total dereliction when I permit tribulation to come upon thee for a season, or suspend the consolations which thou art always fondly desiring; for this is the narrow way to the kingdom of heaven; and it is more expedient for my servants to be exercised with many sufferings, than to enjoy that perpetual rest and delight which they would choose for themselves. I, who know the hidden thoughts of thy heart, and the depth of the evil that is in it, know that thy salvation depends upon thy being sometimes left in the full perception of thy own impotence and wretchedness; lest, in the undisturbed prosperity of the spiritual life, thou shouldst exalt thyself for what is not thy own, and take complacence in vain conceit of perfection, to which man of himself cannot attain. The good I bestow I can both take away and restore again. When I have bestowed it, it is still mine; and when I resume it, I take not away that which is thine; for there is no good of which I am not the principle and centre. When, therefore, I visit thee with adversity, murmur not, neither let thy heart be troubled; for I can soon restore thee to light and peace, and change thy heaviness into joy; but in all my dispensations, acknowledge that I, the Lord, am righteous, and greatly to be praised. If thou wert wise, and didst behold thyself and thy fallen state by that light with which I, who am the truth, enlighten thee, instead of grieving and murmuring at the adversities which befall thee, thou wouldst rejoice and give thanks; nay, thou wouldst "count it all joy thus to endure chastening." I once said to the disciples whom I chose to attend my ministry upon earth, "As the Father hath loved me, so have I loved you;" and I sent them forth into the world, not to luxury, but to conflict; not to honor, but to contempt; not to amusement, but to labor; not to take repose, but to "bring forth much fruit with patience."

TO AN INFANT IN HEAVEN.

THOMAS WARD.

THOU bright and star-like spirit,
  That, in my visions wild,
I see, 'mid heaven's seraphic host,
  O, canst thou be my child?

My grief is quenched in wonder,
  And pride arrests my sighs;
A branch from this unworthy stock
  Now blossoms in the skies.

Our hopes of thee were lofty ;
  But have we cause to grieve ?
O, could our fondest, proudest wish
  A nobler fate conceive ?—

The little weeper tearless,
  The sinner snatched from sin,
The babe to more than manhood grown
  Ere childhood did begin ?

And I, thy earthly teacher,
  Would blush thy powers to see ;
Thou art to me a parent now,
  And I a child to thee.

What bliss is born of sorrow !
  'Tis never sent in vain ;
The heavenly Surgeon maims to save ;
  He gives no useless pain.

Our God, to call us homeward,
  His only Son sent down ;
And now, still more to tempt our hearts,
  Has taken up our own.

GOD THE ONLY SOURCE OF ALL SUPPORT AND CONSOLATION.

DRELINCOURT.

THE only source of all our consolation is God's gracious promise to help us in time of need. Engrave in the bottom of your hearts these divine sayings: When he that hath set his love upon me shall call upon me, I will answer him: I will be with him in trouble; I will deliver him, and honor him. The Lord knoweth how to deliver the godly out of temptations. He is rich unto all that call upon him. He is nigh unto all them that call upon him, to all that call upon him in truth. He fulfils the desires of the humble, he hears their cry. Many are the afflictions of the righteous; but the Lord delivereth him out of them all. Call upon me, saith he, in the day of trouble; I will deliver thee, and thou shalt glorify me. The tenderness of God's love accompanies the glory of his majesty. He is the Father of mercies, and the God of all comfort, *who comforteth us in all our tribulation.* He is that bosom Friend who loveth at all times, as it were a brother who is born for adversity. He is at once the King of kings, and our most cordial Friend. He enters into the house of mourning, and is nigh unto every broken heart and contrite spirit. The lower our estate is, the more he remembereth us. Shall thy God, who loves thee more cordially and with a more unalterable love than the best of fathers, or the most tender-hearted mother, forsake thee in the day of affliction? This merciful and compassionate Father, who took thee into his protection when thou camest into the world, and hath administered to all thy necessities, shall he refuse thee his gracious succor in this thy utmost extremity? He who hath crowned thy youthful days with his divine blessings will not cast thee off when thy strength faileth.

GOD'S KIND CARE OF US.

FRANCIS QUARLES.

EVEN as a nurse, whose child's imperfect pace
Can hardly lead his foot from place to place,
Leaves her fond kissing, sets him down to go,
Nor does uphold him for a step or two,
But when she finds that he begins to fall,
She holds him up, and kisses him withal, —
So God from man *sometimes withdraws his hand*
A while, to teach his infant faith to stand;
But when he sees his feeble strength begin
To fail, he gently takes him up again.

THE FADED ONE.

WILLIS GAYLORD CLARK.

GONE to the slumber which may know no waking
  Till the loud requiem of the world shall swell;
Gone where no sound thy still repose is breaking,
  In a lone mansion through long years to dwell;
Where the sweet gales that herald bud and blossom
  Pour not their music nor their fragrant breath, —
A seal is set upon thy budding bosom,
  A bond of loneliness — a spell of death.

Yet 'twas but yesterday that all before thee
  Shone in the freshness of life's morning hours;
Joy's radiant smile was playing briefly o'er thee,
  And thy light feet impressed but vernal flowers.
The restless spirit charmed thy sweet existence,
  Making all beauteous in Youth's pleasant maze,
While gladsome Hope illumed the onward distance,
  And lit with sunbeams thy expectant days.

How have the garlands of thy childhood withered,
  And Hope's false anthem died upon the air!
Death's cloudy tempests o'er thy way have gathered,
  And his stern bolts have burst in fury there.
On thy pale forehead sleeps the shade of even;
  Youth's braided wreath lies stained in sprinkled dust;
Yet, looking upward in its grief to Heaven,
  Love should not mourn thee, save in hope and trust.

THE DEATH OF THE FLOWERS.

WILLIAM CULLEN BRYANT.

THE melancholy days are come,
  The saddest of the year,
Of wailing winds, and naked woods,
  And meadows brown and sear.
Heaped in the hollows of the grove,
  The withered leaves lie dead ;
They rustle to the eddying gust,
  And to the rabbit's tread.
The robin and the wren are flown,
  And from the shrubs the jay,
And from the wood top caws the crow,
  Through all the gloomy day.

Where are the flowers, the fair young flowers,
  That lately sprang and stood
In brighter light and softer airs,
  A beauteous sisterhood ?
Alas! they all are in their graves ;
  The gentle race of flowers
Are lying in their lowly beds,
  With the fair and good of ours.
The rain is falling where they lie,
  But the cold November rain
Calls not from out the gloomy earth
  The lonely ones again.

The windflower and the violet,
  They perished long ago,
And the brierrose and the orchis died
  Amid the summer glow;
But on the hill the goldenrod,
  And the aster in the wood,
And the yellow sunflower by the brook
  In autumn beauty stood,
Till fell the frost from the clear, cold heaven,
  As falls the plague on men,
And the brightness of their smile was gone,
  From upland, glade, and glen.

And now, when comes the calm, mild day,—
  As still such days will come,—
To call the squirrel and the bee
  From out their winter home;
When the sound of dropping nuts is heard,
  Though all the trees are still,
And twinkle in the smoky light
  The waters of the rill;
The south wind searches for the flowers
  Whose fragrance late he bore,
And sighs to find them in the wood
  And by the streams no more.

And then I think of one who in
  Her youthful beauty died,
The fair, meek blossom that grew up
  And faded by my side;
In the cold, moist earth we laid her,
  When the forest cast the leaf,

And we wept that one so lovely
Should have a life so brief:
Yet not unmeet it was that one
Like that young friend of ours,
So gentle and so beautiful,
Should perish with the flowers.

"There is hope of a tree, if it be cut down, that it will sprout again, and that the tender branches thereof will not cease. Though the root thereof wax old in the earth, and the stock thereof die in the ground, *yet*, through the scent of water, it will bud, and bring forth boughs like a plant. But man dieth, and wasteth away! yea, man giveth up the ghost, and where *is* he? *As* the waters fail from the sea, and the flood decayeth and drieth up, so man lieth down, and riseth not: till the heavens be no more, they shall not awake, nor be raised out of their sleep." — JOB xiv.

"I would not have you to be ignorant, brethren, concerning them which are asleep, that ye sorrow not, even as others which have no hope. For if we believe that Jesus died and rose again, even so them also which sleep in Jesus will God bring with him. . . . For the Lord himself shall descend from heaven with a shout, with the voice of the archangel, and with the trump of God; and the dead in Christ shall rise first." — 1 THESSALONIANS, iv.

A DIRGE.

MRS. HEMANS.

WEEP for the early lost! —
How many flowers were mingled in the crown
Thus, with the lovely, to the grave gone down,
E'en when life promised most!
How many hopes have withered! They that bow
To Heaven's dread will feel all its mysteries now.

Did the young mother's eye
Behold her child, and close upon the day,
Ere from its glance th' awakening spirit's ray
In sunshine could reply?
—Then look for clouds to dim the fairest morn!
O, strong is faith, if woe like this be borne.

For there is hushed on earth
A voice of gladness—there is veiled a face,
Whose parting leaves a dark and silent place
By the once joyous hearth.
A smile hath passed, which filled its home with light,
A soul, whose beauty made that smile so bright!

But there *is* power with faith!
Power, e'en though nature o'er th' untimely grave
Must weep, when God resumes the gem he gave;
For sorrow comes of death,
And with a yearning heart we linger on,
When they whose glance unlocked its founts are gone.

But glory from the dust,
And praise to Him, the merciful, for those
On whose bright memory love may still repose,
With an immortal trust;
Praise for the dead, who leave us, when they part,
Such hope as she hath left—"the pure in heart."

THE LIGHT ABOVE US.

LIFE OF MADAME GUYON.

THERE is a light in yonder skies,
A light unseen by outward eyes;
But clear and bright to inward sense
It shines — the star of Providence.

The radiance of the central throne,
It comes from God, and God alone —
The ray that never yet grew pale,
The star that "shines within the veil."

And faith, unchecked by earthly fears,
Shall lift its eye, though filled with tears,
And while around 'tis dark as night,
Untired shall mark that heavenly light.

THE VOICE OF THE ROD.

REV. THOMAS BROOKS.

As the word hath a voice, the Spirit a voice, and conscience a voice, so the rod hath a voice. Afflictions are the rod of God's anger, the rod of his displeasure, and his rod of revenge : he gives a commission to this rod to awaken, to reform his people, or else to revenge the quarrel of his covenant upon them, if they will not hear, and kiss the rod, and sit mute and silent under it. "The Lord's voice crieth unto the city, and the man of wisdom shall see thy name; hear ye the rod, and who hath appointed it." (Mic. iv. 9.) God's rods are not mutes; they are speaking as well as smiting; every twig hath a voice. Ah, soul, saith one twig, thou sayest it smarts; well, tell me, is it good provoking a jealous God? (Jer. iv. 18.) Ah, soul, saith another twig, thou sayest it is bitter, it reacheth to thy heart; but hath not thine own doings procured these things? (Rom. iv. 21.) Ah, soul, saith another twig, where is the profit, the pleasure, that you have found in wandering from God? (Hos. iii. 7.) Ah, soul, saith another twig, was it not best with you when you were high in your communion with God, and humble and close in your walking with God? (Mic. iv. 8.) Ah, Christian, saith another twig, wilt thou search thy heart, and try thy ways, and turn to the Lord thy God? (Lam. iii. 40.) Ah, soul, saith another twig, wilt thou die to sin more than ever? (Rom. xiv. 7, 8;) and to the world more than ever? (Gal. vi. 14;) and to relations more than ever, and to thyself more than ever? Ah, soul, saith another twig, wilt thou live more to Christ, and cleave closer to Christ, and prize Christ more, and venture further for Christ than ever? Ah, soul, saith another twig, wilt thou love Christ with a more inflamed love, and hope in Christ with a more raised hope, and depend upon Christ with a greater confidence, and wait upon Christ with more invincible patience? Now, if the soul be not mute and silent under the rod, how is it possible that it should ever hear the voice of the rod, or that it should ever hearken to the voice of every twig of the rod? The rod hath a voice that is in the hands of earthly fathers; but children understand it not, till they are hushed and quiet, and brought to kiss it, and sit silently under it: no more shall we hear or understand the voice of the rod that is in our heavenly Father's hand, till we come to kiss it, and sit silently under it.

DIRGE.

MISS LANDON.

LAY her in the gentle earth,
Where the summer maketh mirth,
Where young violets have birth,
    Where the lily bendeth.
Lay her there, the lovely one,
With the rose her funeral stone,
And for tears such showers alone
    As the rain of April lendeth.

From the midnight's quiet hour
Will come dews of holy power
O'er the sweetest human flower
    That was ever loved.
But she was too fair and dear
For our troubled pathway here;
Heaven, that was her natural sphere,
    Has its own removed.

"We are forbidden to murmur, but we are not forbidden to regret; and whom we love tenderly while living we may still pursue with an affectionate remembrance, without having any occasion to charge ourselves with rebellion against the sovereignty that appointed a separation."—COWPER.

O, STAY THOSE TEARS.

ANDREWS NORTON.

O, STAY thy tears! for they are blest
  Whose days are past, whose toil is done:
Here midnight care disturbs our rest,
  Here sorrow dims the noonday sun.

For laboring virtue's anxious toil,
  For patient sorrow's stifled sigh,
For faith that marks the conqueror's spoil,
  Heaven grants the recompense — to die.

How blest are they whose transient years
  Pass like an evening meteor's flight!
Not dark with guilt, nor dim with tears;
  Whose course is short, unclouded, bright.

How cheerless were our lengthened way,
  Did Heaven's own light not break the gloom,
Stream downward from eternal day,
  And cast a glory round the tomb!

Then stay thy tears; the blest above
  Have hailed a spirit's heavenly birth,
Sung a new song of joy and love;
  And why should anguish reign on earth?

A CONSOLATORY LETTER.

MRS. ISABELLA GRAHAM.

When the Christian suffers the loss of a near and dear friend, who, to his knowledge, has given no reasonable evidence of a hope in Christ, his case seems almost beyond the reach of consolation; and, while feeling the bitterness of his twofold affliction, he is ready to exclaim, "My stroke is heavier than my groaning." The following letter, to a sadly-bereaved mother, from the pen of Mrs. Isabella Graham, is given for those suffering under such deep heart grief.

THERE are cases to which God alone can speak; afflictions which he *alone* can console. Such are those under which the sufferer is commanded to be "still and know that he is God." He never leaves his people in any case, but sometimes shuts them up from human aid. Their grief is too great to be consoled by human tongue or pen. Such I have experienced. I lost my only son; I neither know when nor where; and, for any thing I know, in a state of rebellion against God. Here, at my heart, it lies still: who can speak to me of it? Neither can I reason upon it. Aaron held his peace. Old Eli said, "It is the Lord; let him do what seemeth good in his sight." Samuel, in his turn, had his heart wrung by his ungodly son. David lamented over his beloved Absalom; but it availed him nothing. Job's sons and daughters were all cut off in one day; he himself lay in deep, sore, bodily affliction; his friends sat seven days and seven nights without opening their mouths, because they saw his affliction was very great; and if they spoke, it was to aggravate it; and when God himself spoke, he gave him no reason for his dealings, but charged him with folly and madness. "Shall he that contendeth with the Almighty instruct him? He that reproveth God, let him answer it." Then he laid his hand on his mouth, confessed himself vile, and became dumb before God; abhorring himself, and repenting in dust and ashes, instead of the splendid catalogue of virtues enumerated in chapter twenty-nine, and complaints in chapter ten, which I make not the least doubt were true, as far as human virtue can reach; but if God charge "even his angels with folly," shall man, corrupt, self-destroyed man, plead merit before God?

But, my dear friend, I do not find in all God's Bible any thing requiring us to acquiesce in the final destruction of any for whom we have prayed, pleaded, and committed to him; least of all our offspring, whom he has commanded us to train up for him. "Children are God's heritage." I do not say he has given us any promise for the obstinately wicked; but when cut off, he only requires us to *be still*, to hold our peace. I do not think he takes hope from us. God has set limits to our *faith* for others; our faith must not rest in opposition to his threatenings. We must believe that "the wicked shall be turned into hell, and all that forget God;" but he has set no bounds to his own mercy; in that glorious plan of redemption, by which he substitutes his own Son in the stead of sinners, he has made provision for the chief of sinners, and can now be just and consistent while he justifies the ungodly who believe in Jesus. Short was the time between the thief's petition and the promise of salvation; nay, the petition was the earnest of it. The same was the case with the jailer; I think, too, the publican had the earnest in his petition. Now, instead of laboring to bring my mind to acquiesce in the condemnation of my child, on the supposition of its being for God's glory, I try to be *still*, as he has commanded; not to follow my child to the yet invisible world; but turning my eyes to that character which God has revealed of himself—to the plan of redemption—to the sovereignty of God in the execution of that plan—to his names of grace, "The Lord, the Lord God, merciful and gracious, slow to anger, abundant in goodness and truth, forgiving iniquity, and transgression, and sin," while he adds, "and that will by no means clear the guilty," I meet it with his own declaration, "He hath made Him to be sin for us who knew no sin, that we might be made the righteousness of God in him." I read also that "mercy rejoiceth against judgment," and many other like Scriptures, which, although I dare not ground a belief of his salvation on them, afford one ray of hope after another, that God may have made him a monument of mercy to the glory of his grace.

Thus God himself consoles his own praying people, while man ought to be very cautious, if not silent, where the Scriptures are silent, as it respects the final state of another, whose heart we cannot know, nor what God may have wrought in it. God hath set bounds to our faith, which can nowhere find solid ground to fix upon but on his own written promise. Yet, as I said above, he has set no bounds to his own mercy, and he has made provision for its boundless flow, as far as he shall please to extend it, through the atonement and merits of his own Son, "who is able to save to the uttermost all who come unto God by him." Now, my dear friend, you have my ideas of our situation; if they be correct, I pray that our compassionate Father may comfort you by them; if otherwise, may he pardon what is amiss, and lead you and myself to such consolation as he himself will own as the work of his Spirit, and save us from the enemy of our own spirit.

GOD A REFUGE IN TRIALS.

BEDDOME.

My times of sorrow and of joy,
  Great God, are in thy hand;
My choicest comforts come from thee,
  And go at thy command.

If thou shouldst take them all away,
  Yet would I not repine;
Before they were possessed by me
  They were entirely thine.

Nor would I drop a murmuring word,
  Though all the world were gone,

But seek enduring happiness
In thee, and thee alone.

"When thou art in tribulation, and all these things are come upon thee, even in the later days, if thou turn to the Lord thy God, and shalt be obedient unto his voice, (for the Lord thy God is a merciful God,) he will not forsake thee, neither destroy thee."—DEUTERONOMY iv.

REMINISCENCES.

MONTGOMERY.

WHERE are ye with whom in life I started,
Dear companions of my golden days?
Ye are dead, estranged from me, or parted,
Flown, like morning clouds, a thousand ways.

Where art thou, in youth my friend and brother,
Yea, in soul my friend and brother still?
Heaven received thee, and on earth none other
Can the void in this lorn bosom fill.

Where is she whose looks were love and gladness?
Love and gladness I no longer see!
She is gone; and since that hour of sadness,
Nature seems her sepulchre to me.

Where am I?—life's current, faintly flowing,
Brings the welcome warning of release;
Struck with death, ah, whither am I going?
All is well—my spirit parts in peace.

WEEP NOT FOR THE PAST.

Weep not for the past; 'tis a dream that is fled;
Its sunshine has vanished, its garlands are dead;
Deep, deep in its shadows bright hopes are laid low;
O, call them not back to the land whence they go.
They came as the light that may gleam from on high,
From the wing of some spirit that passes us by,
So gently, we deemed that the fetters of earth
Had fallen away for a holier birth;
And they passed — but a voice lingers yet on the ear
In accents that fall from some sunnier sphere,
"*Weep not, child of sorrow, for hopes that were thine;*
Unblest are the gifts of an UNHALLOWED *shrine.*
Thy idol was earthly — thy life star has set;
Bright stars are in HEAVEN, *that beam for thee yet!*"
Weep not for the past, though it hold in its gloom
Loved forms that have sunk to their rest in the tomb,
Fond voices that rang in the laugh of the song,
And faces that smiled as they flitted along;
O, call them not back! for they went in their mirth,
Ere their hearts had been chilled by one frost of this earth;
And 'tis sweet to lie down with the song yet unsung,
And wake its first notes in a heavenly tongue!

Then yield not to sorrow ; life has not a day
That gives not some sunbeam to lighten our way ;
But cull from the past, from each blessing that dies,
A gem to illumine the crown for the skies.
The future is o'er us ; the present is ours,
To shroud it in sadness, or gild it with flowers ;
To sink on life's ocean, or find on its wave
A halo that wakes e'en the gloom of the grave.

CHRISTIAN RESIGNATION.

HANNAH MORE.

THE pagan philosophers have given many admirable precepts, both for resigning blessings and for sustaining misfortunes; but wanting the motives and sanctions of Christianity, though they excite much intellectual admiration, they produce little practical effect. The stars which glittered in their moral night, though bright, imparted no warmth. Their most beautiful dissertations on death had no charm to extract its sting. We receive no support from their most elaborate treatises on immortality, for want of Him who "brought life and immortality to light." Their consolatory discussion could not strip the grave of its terrors, for to them it was not "swallowed up in victory." To conceive of the soul as an immortal principle, without proposing a scheme for the pardon of its sins, was but cold consolation. Their future state was but a happy guess, their heaven but a fortunate conjecture.

When we peruse their finest composition, we admire the manner in which the medicine is administered, but we do not find it effectual for the cure, nor even for the mitigation, of our disease. The beauty of the sentiment we applaud, but our heart continues to ache. There is no healing balm in their elegant prescription. These four little words, "*Thy will be done*," contain a charm of more powerful efficacy than all the discipline of the stoic school! They cut up a long train of clear but cold reasoning, and supersede whole volumes of argument on fate and necessity.

What sufferer ever derived any ease from the subtile distinction of the hair-splitting casuist, who allowed "that pain was very, very troublesome," but resolved never to acknowledge it to be an evil? . . . He does not directly say that pain is not an evil, but by a sophistical turn professes that philosophy will never *confess* it to be an evil. But what consolation does the sufferer draw from the quibbling nicety? "What difference is there," as Archbishop Tillotson well inquires, "between things being troublesome and being evils, when all the evil of an affliction lies in the trouble it creates to us?" Christianity knows none of these fanciful distinctions. She never pretends to insist that pain is not an evil, but she does more; she converts it into a good. Christianity, therefore, teaches a fortitude as much more noble than philosophy, as meeting pain with resignation to the hand that inflicts it is more heroic than denying it to be an evil.

To submit on the mere human ground that there is no alternative is not resignation, but hopelessness. To bear affliction solely because impatience will not remove it is but an inferior, though a just reason for bearing it. It savors rather of despair than submission when not sanctioned by a higher principle. "It is the Lord; let him do what seemeth him good," is at once a motive of more powerful obligation than all the documents which philosophy ever suggested, a firmer ground of support than all the energies that natural fortitude ever supplied.

Under any visitation, God permits us to think the affliction "not joyous, but grievous." But though he allows us to feel, we must not allow ourselves to repine. There is a sort of heroism in bearing up against affliction, which some adopt on the ground that it raises their character, and confers dignity on their suffering. This philosophic firmness is far from being the temper which Christianity inculcates.

When we are compelled by the hand of God to endure sufferings, or driven by a conviction of the vanity of the world to renounce its enjoyments, we must not endure the one on the low principle of its being inevitable; nor, in flying from the other, must we retire to the contemplation of our own virtues. We must not, with a sullen intrepidity, collect ourselves into a centre of our own — into a cold apathy to all without, and a proud approbation of all within. We must not contract our scattered faults into a sort of dignified selfishness, nor concentrate our feelings into a proud magnanimity; we must not adopt an independent rectitude. A gloomy stoicism is not Christian heroism.

A melancholy non-resistance is not Christian resignation.

Nor must we indemnify ourselves for our outward self-control by secret murmurings. We may be admired for our resolution in this instance, as for our generosity and disinterestedness in other instances; but we deserve little commendation for whatever we give up, if we do not give up our own inclination. It is inward repining that we must endeavor to repress; it is the discontent of the heart, the unexpressed, but not unfelt murmur, against which we must pray for grace and struggle for resistance. It is the hidden rebellion of the will we must subdue, if we would submit as Christians. Nor must we justify our impatience by saying that, if our affliction did not disqualify us from being useful to our families, and active in the service of God, we could more cheerfully bear it. Let us rather be assured that it does not disqualify us for that duty which we most need, and to which God calls us by the very disqualification. In times of affliction we must summon all the fortitude of the rational being, all the resignation of the Christian. The principles we have been learning must now be made practical. The speculations we have admired we must now realize. All that we have been studying was in order to furnish materials for this grand exigency. All the strength we have been collecting must now be brought into action. We must now draw to a point all the scattered arguments, all the several motives, all the individual supports, all the cheering promises of religion. We must exemplify all the rules we have given to others; we must embody all the resolutions we have formed for ourselves; we must reduce our precepts to experience; we must pass from discourses on submission to its exercise; from dissertations on suffering to sustaining it. We must recollect what we have said of the supports of faith and hope when our strength was in full vigor, when our heart was at ease, and our mind undisturbed. Let us collect all our mental strength. Let us implore the aid of holy hope and fervent faith, to show that religion is not a beautiful theory, but a soul-sustaining truth. . . . The strongest faith is wanted in the hardest trials. Under those trials, to the confirmed Christian, the highest degree of grace is commonly imparted. . . .

The reflecting Christian will consider affliction the consequence and punishment of moral evil. He will mourn not only that he suffers pain, but because that pain is the effect of sin. If man had not sinned, he would not have suffered. Our merciful Father has no pleasure in the sufferings of his children; he chastens them in love; he never inflicts a stroke he could safely spare; he inflicts it to purify as well as to punish, to caution as well as to cure, to improve as well as to chastise.

What a support to reflect that the Captain of our salvation was made perfect through sufferings; that if we suffer with him, we shall also reign with him — which implies also the reverse, that if we do not suffer with him, we shall not reign with him; that is, if we suffer merely because we cannot help it, without reference to him, without suffering for his sake and in his spirit! If it be not sanctified suffering, it will avail but little. We shall not be paid for having suffered, as is the creed of too many, but our meetness for the kingdom of glory will be increased if we suffer according to his will and after his example. . . .

Under the most severe visitations, let us compare our own sufferings with the cup which our Redeemer drank for our sakes — drank to avert the divine displeasure from us. . . . He was deserted in his most trying hour ; deserted, probably, by those whose limbs, sight, life he had restored, whose souls he had come to save. We are surrounded by unwearied friends ; every pain is mitigated by sympathy. . . . When *our* souls are "exceeding sorrowful," *our* friends participate our sorrow — forsaking us not in our "agony," but sympathizing where they cannot relieve! Besides this, we must acknowledge, with the penitent malefactor, "We indeed suffer justly, but this man hath done nothing amiss." We suffer for our offences the inevitable penalty of our fallen nature. He bore *our* sins, and those of the whole human race. Hence the heart-rending interrogation, "Is it nothing to you all, ye that pass by? Behold and see if there be any sorrow like unto my sorrow, which is done unto me, wherewith the Lord hath afflicted me in the day of his fierce anger." How cheering to reflect that he not only suffered for us then, but is sympathizing with us now! that "in all our afflictions he is afflicted"! The tenderness of the sympathy seems to add a value to the sacrifice, while the vastness of the sacrifice endears the sympathy by ennobling it.

How many motives has the Christian to restrain his murmurs! Murmuring offends God, both as it is injurious to his goodness, and as it perverts the occasion which God has now offered for giving an example of patience. Let us not complain that we have nothing to do when we are furnished with the opportunity, as well as called to the duty, of resignation ; the duty, indeed, is always ours, but the occasion is now more eminently given. Let us not say, even in this depressed state, that we have nothing to be thankful for.

RESIGNATION.

H. W. LONGFELLOW.

THERE is no flock, however watched and tended,
  But one dead lamb is there ;
There is no fireside, howsoe'er defended,
  But has one vacant chair.

The air is full of farewells to the dying,
  And mournings for the dead :
The heart of Rachel, for her children crying,
  Will not be comforted.

Let us be patient : these severe afflictions
  Not from the ground arise,
But oftentimes celestial benedictions
  Assume this dark disguise.

We see but dimly through the mists and vapors;
  Amid these earthly damps,
What seem to us but dim funereal tapers
  May be heaven's distant lamps.

There is no death: what seems so is transition:
  This life of mortal breath
Is but a suburb of the life elysian,
  Whose portals we call death.

She is not dead, — the child of our affection, —
  But gone unto that school
Where she no longer needs our poor protection,
  And Christ himself doth rule.

In that great cloister's stillness and seclusion,
  By guardian angels led,
Safe from temptation, safe from sin's pollution,
  She lives whom we call dead.

Day after day we think what she is doing
  In those bright realms of air;
Year after year her tender steps pursuing,
  Behold her grown more fair.

Thus do we walk with her, and keep unbroken
  The bond which nature gives,
Thinking that our remembrance, though unspoken,
  May reach her where she lives.

Not as a child shall we again behold her;
  For when, with raptures wild,

In our embraces we again infold her,
  She will not be a child.

But a fair maiden in her Father's mansion,
  Clothed with celestial grace,
And beautiful with all the soul's expansion
  Shall we behold her face.

And though at times, impetuous with emotion,
  And anguish long suppressed,
The swelling heart heaves moaning like the ocean
  That cannot be at rest, —

We will be patient, and assuage the feeling
  We cannot wholly stay;
By silence sanctifying, not concealing,
  The grief that must have way.

"There is an immeasurable distance between submission to the cross and acceptance of it. Simon the Cyrenian compelled to bear it, and Paul glorying in his infirmities that the power of Christ might rest on him, are the representatives of two classes whom man may confound, but who are severally discerned of God. The one bends in silent acquiescence beneath the burden that a stronger hand has fixed beyond his power to shake off; the other regards his affliction as a Heaven-appointed means of bringing him to a fuller participation in what Christ's sufferings have purchased for him — even that strength proportioned to his day which is doubly precious as being a fulfilled promise." — CHARLOTTE ELIZABETH.

A BELIEF IN A SUPERINTENDING PROVIDENCE THE ONLY ADEQUATE SUPPORT UNDER AFFLICTION.

WORDSWORTH.

ONE adequate support
For the calamities of mortal life
Exists, one only — an assured belief
That the procession of our fate, howe'er
Sad or disturbed, is ordered by a Being
Of infinite benevolence and power;
Whose everlasting purposes embrace
All accidents, converting them to good.
The darts of anguish *fix* not where the seat
Of suffering hath been thoroughly fortified
By acquiescence in the Will Supreme,
For time and for eternity; by faith,
Faith absolute in God, including hope,
And the defence that lies in boundless love
Of his perfections; with habitual dread
Of aught unworthily conceived, endured
Impatiently; ill done, or left undone,
To the dishonor of his holy name.
Soul of our souls, and safeguard of the world,
Sustain — thou only canst — the sick of heart;
Restore their languid spirits, and recall
Their lost affections unto thee and thine!

. . . . .

'Tis, by comparison, an easy task
Earth to despise; but to converse with Heaven—
This is not easy: to relinquish all
We have, or hope, of happiness and joy,
And stand in freedom loosened from this world,
I deem not arduous; but must needs confess
That 'tis a thing impossible to frame
Conceptions equal to the soul's desires,
And the most difficult of tasks to *keep*
Heights which the soul is competent to gain.
Man is of dust; ethereal hopes are his,
Which, when they should sustain themselves aloft,
Want due consistence; like a pillar of smoke,
That with majestic energy from earth
Rises, but, having reached the thinner air,
Melts, and dissolves, and is no longer seen.
From this infirmity of mortal kind
Sorrow proceeds, which else were not; at least,
If grief be something hallowed and ordained,
If, in proportion, it be just and meet,
Through this, 'tis able to maintain its hold,
In that excess which conscience disapproves.
For who could sink and settle to that point
Of selfishness? so senseless who could be
In framing estimates of loss and gain,
As long and perseveringly to mourn
For any object of his love, removed
From this unstable world, if he could fix
A satisfying view upon that state
Of pure, imperishable blessedness,
Which reason promises and holy writ
Insures to all believers? Yet mistrust

Is of such incapacity, methinks,
No natural branch; despondency far less.
And, if there be whose tender frames have drooped
Even to the dust, apparently, through weight
Of anguish unrelieved, and lack of power
An agonizing sorrow to transmute,
Infer not hence a hope from those withheld
When wanted most; a confidence impaired
So pitiably, that, having ceased to see
With bodily eyes, they are borne down by love
Of what is lost, and perish through regret.
O, no; full oft the innocent sufferer sees
Too clearly, feels too vividly, and longs
To realize the vision with intense
And over-constant yearning; there, there lies
The excess, by which the balance is destroyed.
Too, too contracted are these walls of flesh,
This vital warmth too cold, these visual orbs,
Though inconceivably endowed, too dim
For any passion of the soul that leads
To ecstasy; and, all the crooked paths
Of time and change disdaining, takes its course
Along the line of limitless desires.
I, speaking now from such disorder free,
Nor rapt, nor craving, but in settled peace,
I cannot doubt that they whom you deplore
Are glorified; or, if they sleep, shall wake
From sleep, and dwell with God in endless love.
Hope, below this, consists not with belief
In mercy, carried infinite degrees
Beyond the tenderness of human hearts:
Hope, below this, consists not with belief

In perfect wisdom, guiding mightiest power,
That finds no limits but her own pure will.

But, above all, the victory is most sure
For him who, seeking faith by virtue, strives
To yield entire submission to the law
Of conscience ; conscience reverenced and obeyed
As God's most intimate presence in the soul,
And his most perfect image in the world.
Endeavor thus to live ; these rules regard ;
These helps solicit ; and a steadfast seat
Shall then be yours among the happy few
Who dwell on earth, yet breathe empyreal air,—
Sons of the morning. For your nobler part,
Ere disencumbered of her mortal chains,
Doubt shall be quelled, and trouble chased away ;
With only such degree of sadness left
As may support longings of pure desire,
And strengthen love, rejoicing secretly
In the sublime attractions of the grave.

REASONS AGAINST IMMODERATE SORROW.

SYMON PATRICK, D. D.

FOR whose sake dost thou weep? For the sake of him that is dead, or for thy own? Not for him that is dead, sure, for we suppose him to be happy. Is it reasonable to say, Ah me, what shall I do? I have lost a dear friend that shall eat and drink no more. Alas! he shall never hunger again; never be sick again; never be vexed and troubled; and, which is more, he shall never die again. Yet this is the frantic language of our tears, if we weep for the sake of him that is gone. Suppose thy friend should come to thee, and shake thee by the hand, and say, My good friend, why dost thou lament, and afflict thy soul? I am gone to the paradise of God, a sight most beautiful to be beheld, and more rare to be enjoyed. To that paradise am I flown, where there is nothing but joy and triumph, nothing but friendship and endless love. There am I, where the Head of us all is, and where we enjoy the light of his most blessed face. I would not live, if I might, again; no, not for the love of thee. I have no such affection to thy society—once most dear unto me—that I would exchange my present company to hold commerce with thee. But do thou rather come hither as soon as thou canst. And bid thy friends that they mourn not for thee when thou diest, unless they would wish thee to be miserable again.

If we should have such a short converse with one of our acquaintance, what should we think? what should we say? Should we fall a mourning and crying again? Would it open a new sluice for our tears to flow out? Would we pray him to go to heaven no more, but stay with us? Would we entreat him to beg of God that he might come and comfort us? If not, then let us be well content, unless we can give a better reason for our immoderate tears than our love to him.

Holcoth* reports of a learned man that was found dead in his study with his book before him: a friend of his was exceedingly amazed at the sight when he first came into the room; but when he looked a little further, he found his fore finger pointing at this place in the Book of Wisdom, chapter 4, verse 7: "But though the righteous be prevented with death, yet shall he be in rest." And when he observed this, he was as much comforted as he was before dejected. We have no reason to lament them who are made immortal, and that live with God. If we respect them only, we should carry them forth as the Egyptians did the great prophet of Isis when he died,† not with howlings and sorrow, but with hymns and joy, as being made an heir with our betters, and gone to possess most glorious things.

The truth of it is, if it were rational love to him that expresseth these tears, then we should not begin them so soon, nor make such a noise, nor cry, when men are dying. For the sad countenances and the miserable lamentations wherewith we encompass sick men's beds make death seem more frightful to them than it is in itself. What misery am I falling into — may a man think — that causes them to make such a moan? What is this death, that makes even them look so ghastly who are not like to die? What a mischief is it to leave so many sad hearts behind me, and to go myself — it should seem by them — to some sad and dismal place also! I tell you, a dying man had need have a double courage to look both death and them in the faces, or else their indiscrete shrieks and

* In 4 Sap. 5, 7.

† Heloid. 1, 7, Æthiop.

lamentations will make a poor soul fall into such dark and cloudy thoughts. Men are fain, therefore, to say that it is indeed love to themselves that forces them thus to bemoan the death of their friends. But what are you, that cannot be contented one should be made much better by making of you a little worse? Is this the great love you pretend to your friend, that you are extremely sorry he is gone to heaven. Are you a friend, that look more at your own small benefit than at his great gain? Was he not much beholden to you for your love, that would have had him lived till you were dead, that he might have been so miserable in mourning for you, as you think now yourselves to be? . . .

But how doth it appear that mere self-love is the original of these tears? Suppose this person to have been at so wide a distance from us for a year or two, that no tidings of him could come to us. Did we weep and lament all that while because he was not with us? Did not the thoughts that he lived, and hopes to see him again, comfort us? And yet, was he not then in a manner dead, when we neither saw, nor felt, nor heard from him? What help did we receive from him at that distance? or wherein did he pleasure us? If we did not account ourselves so miserable all that time as to spend it in tears, we ought not to do it now. We are now as we were then; in all things the very same, save only in the knowledge that he is dead. But was he not dead, as I said, to us before? Was he not like a man in another world? What was there that he did for us which we do not now receive at his hands? Let us be as quiet now as we would have been on such an occasion; especially since we know our friend still lives, and we have hope to see him again. Natural affection, I confess, in either case will make us big with sighs, and burst forth often into tears. We feel we are not as we were before. There is something wanting which we formerly enjoyed. And it is an old friend, perhaps, which *nature* cannot but be loath to part withal. Get a new nature, then, and that will mend all. Though the first motions be so free that they owe no tribute to reason, yet, when they come, we shall be careful not to follow them; if we do, it will not be very far. Religion and reason, if we hearken to them, will teach us to restrain ourselves. "Religion," as a great person speaks, "will not suffer us not to will what God wills. And reason will teach us to bear those things with an equal mind which do not happen to us alone, and which we cannot by all our tears make not to have happened." They will not let us expect that time should take away this sickness from us. That is the remedy of vulgar spirits: *Sapientis est, tempus ipsum antevenire, et dolori ipsi nascenti occurrere* — it is the part of a wise man to outstrip time, and get before it; to prevent a grief that is growing, and strangle it in the very birth. And, indeed, from hence we conclude that it is not mere natural affection either to which we commonly owe our sadness and sorrows, but the freshness and presence of the cause of them. For time, as was said, will make us forget them; or if our parents had died a little after we were born, we should never have wept, when we came of age, to think that they were departed. It is no hard matter, then, for a considerate person to cease his grief, seeing it depends upon such small causes. And if one shall say that it is love to the good of the world that makes him mourn for the loss of a useful person, he hath reason to rejoice that he loves the good of men so much. For then he will labor to do much good in the world himself; and he will persuade all the friends he hath remaining, that they would do all the good they can, and repair that loss.

If he were a *good* man, then thou needest not mourn now, for thou mayst hope to see him again, if thou art good. Thus thou mayst comfort thyself: My friend is not gone, but gone before. He is separated from us, but not lost. He is absent, but not dead. He hath taken a journey into a far country, and there I may go to see him. What matter is it whether my friend return to me, or I go to him? None but this — that if he be in a better place, then it is better that I go to see him than that he come to see me. Should we not desire to be better ourselves, and not to have him made worse? Then let us contentedly follow as fast as we can, hoping there where he is to embrace again. We cannot expect him in our house, but he expects us in his. He cannot come down to us, but we may go up to him. He cannot come back, but we may follow after. And there is no difference, as I said, between his visiting of us at our home, and our going to see him at his, but only this — that it is a great deal better for us to see him there where he is, and not where we are now ourselves. Let us not mourn, therefore, for that which cannot be, but rejoice for that which may and will be. And let it comfort us that we shall come together again, but in a better place than we would have it; we shall have our desires fulfilled, but in a more excellent manner than we desire. And if, in the mean time, he can do us any good, we may be sure that we shall not want it. . . . Think, then, of the time past, and rejoice that thou didst find so sweet a friend. Imagine not how long thou mightst have enjoyed him, but think how long thou didst. It was but natural to lose him; but it was supernatural to enjoy him. All men are born to die, but all men are not born to live so long before they die. All men have acquaintance, but all men have not friends. Therefore he that hath a friend, and hath him so long, is to acknowledge that God is very much his Friend. He was not ours, but was given us by God; or rather, he was not given, but only lent. We had not the propriety, but only the use. We have not lost any thing that was our own, but only restored that which was another's. And, therefore, now that he is taken away, we are not to be angry that God requires his own, but to be thankful that he hath lent us so long that which was none of our own. And assure yourselves there is nothing more unreasonable than to mourn that God gave us a thing no longer, and not to rejoice that he gave us that which is so desirable at all. Cease your tears, I beseech you, unless you will show that you deserved to have wept a little sooner. Either say that he was not worth the having, and then you need not weep at all, or else give God the thanks that you had a person so worthy, and that will stay your immoderate weeping. . . . When you are apt to fetch a sigh, and say, O, my dear friend is gone! call it in again, and say, Thanks be to God that I had such a one to lose. Who would not be willing to spend some tears after so much joy? But then the remembrance of the joy will command that the tears do not overflow. It is an excellent saying of Seneca, "I ever think of my friends with joy; for I had them as if I should lose them, and I have lost them as if I had them." If we could but think of them as dying while they are alive, then we should more easily think of them as alive when they are dead. If we could be willing to part with them when we have them, we should think that we have them when we have parted with them. And the truth is, we cannot please ourselves long in the remembrance of them, unless it be accompanied with some joy. I do not advise you to forget your friends, and put them out of mind, but to remember them, and keep them in your thoughts. But how short a remembrance, saith the same Seneca, must that be, which is always joined with grief and sorrow! If we would remember one always, we must remember him with pleasure; for no man will return willingly to that which he cannot think of without his torment. And if there be any little grief intermixed with our thoughts, yet that grief hath its pleasure. As the sharpness of old wine doth make it more acceptable to men's palates, and as apples are more grateful for their sour sweetness, so Attalus was wont to say, that the remembrance of our friends is the more pleasant for that little sorrow that is mingled with it. . . .

Ask thyself, Who is it that governs the world? Is it the will of God, or thy will, that thou prayest may be done? Shall not he that made a thing have leave to dispose of it as he thinks good? By what law is it that he shall not do what he pleases with his own?

Must we have our wills in all things, and must not he have his will also? Must not he be pleased as well as we? If we think it so reasonable to have what we will, then it is more reasonable that he should have what pleases him. Now, if our will and his will cannot stand together, which shall bend and submit themselves to the other? Is not his will most wise? If he had considered better, would he have done otherwise? Could we have told him what would be most fit for us? If we had been of his counsel, should not this friend have been taken away? Doth he will things because he will? Perhaps there is no reason at all for our wills, and we are in love with a thing we know not why. Shall we think that he is so in like manner? Or, if we have any reasons, are not his better? We would have the life of a child, that he may be a comfort unto us: God will have us to part with him, that he himself may be our only comfort. We should choose his life, that he might enjoy the things that we have got; but God thinks fit that he should die, that we may put our estates to better uses, whereby we are assured he may be more glorified. Or perhaps we desire our children may live for God's glory's sake, that they may honor and serve him in the world. But cannot he tell what is best for his own glory? Is he so careless of that as to take away the things without which he cannot be served? Let us, then, cease our complaints, unless we would have him to let us govern the world. . . .

Doth not God do all things for our good? Do we wish better to ourselves than God doth? Hath not he the greatest care of all his creatures, to see that it be well with them? Did he make them for any other end than that they might be happy? Is there the least sparrow that falls to the ground without our Father's providence? Then mankind must needs be under a greater love, and none of them can die by chance, but by his direction. And, above all other men, he hath a singular care over the persons of good Christians, the very hairs of whose heads are all numbered. If not so much as a hair can drop off without him, much less can any body of them fall into their graves but he hath a hand in it. But still he hath a more special providence over such Christians as are fatherless and widows, helpless, and destitute of all succor. And, therefore, as it was his goodness that took their friends away, so much more will his goodness take care of them whom he hath left none else to take care of. He considers us not only as his children, but as children placed in the midst of such and such circumstances, as desolate and sad, as left only to his providence and tuition. And therefore it is that the Psalmist saith, "Thou art the helper of the fatherless." (Ps. x. 14.) And, in another place, "A father of the fatherless, and a judge of the widows, is God in his holy habitation." (Ps. lxviii. 5.) "I am poor and sorrowful; let thy salvation, O God, set me up on high." (Ps. lxix. 29.) Yea, and all good men are full of compassion to such persons; so that "the blessing of those who are ready to perish" comes upon them, and they cause "the widow's heart to sing for joy." (Job xxix. 13.)

It is an excellent saying of the royal philosopher Antoninus, worthy to be engraven upon our minds, "If there be a God, then nothing can be hurtful to us, for he will not involve us in evil. But if either there be none, or he take no care of men's matters, what shall I live for in a world that is without a God, or without a providence? But there is a God, and he cares for men also, and hath put it into their power not to fall into those things which are truly evil. And for the rest that befall us, if any thing of them had been evil, he would have provided that we should have been able not to have fallen into that either." But if this great person had known, also, that God leaves us not alone to our own power, when he sends any thing upon us, but that he hath a peculiar love to his servants when they are in trouble, and affords them his assistance, he would have said on this sort: "If we be not alone without God, then nothing need discomfort us, for he is the God of all comfort. If we be alone, then we had need to be most discomforted for that, and never endure in a condition without God. But we are not alone, and we are least alone when we are alone; and have him most when we have other things least. Therefore he hath put it into our power not to be troubled, but to go to him for comfort in all that befalls us; and if there were no comfort in him for us in such cases, then they should not have befallen us. Let us not, therefore, mourn as long as we have a God, and as long as all things make us seek for our comfort in him."

SUBMISSION TO AFFLICTIONS.

SWAINE.

There is a secret in the ways of God,
With his own children, which none others know,
That sweetens all he does ; and if such peace,
While under his afflicting hand, we find,
What will it be to see him as he is,
And past the reach of all that now disturbs
The tranquil soul's repose ? to contemplate,
In retrospect unclouded, all the means
By which his wisdom has prepared his saints
For the vast weight of glory which remains?
Come, then, Affliction, if my Father bids,
And be my frowning friend: a friend that frowns
Is better than a smiling enemy.

PRAISE FOR AFFLICTIONS.

CAROLINE FRY.

For what shall I praise thee, my God and my King?
For what blessings the tribute of gratitude bring ?
Shall I praise thee for pleasure, for health, or for ease?
For the spring of delight and the sunshine of peace ?

Shall I praise thee for flowers that bloom on my breast?
For joys in perspective, and pleasures possessed?
For the spirits that brightened my days of delight,
And the slumbers that sat on my pillow by night?

For this I should praise thee; but only for this,
I should leave half untold the donation of bliss:
I thank thee for sickness, for sorrow, for care,
For the thorns I have gathered, the anguish I bear;—

For nights of anxiety, watchings, and tears,
A present of pain, a perspective of fears:
I praise thee, I bless thee, my King and my God,
For the good and the evil thy hand hath bestowed.

The flowers were sweet, but their fragrance is flown;
They yielded no fruit; they are withered and gone:
The thorn it was poignant, but precious to me;
'Twas the message of mercy—it led me to thee.

"It is with the wind and storm of tribulation that God, in the garner of the soul, separates the true wheat from the chaff. Always remember, therefore, that God comes to thee in thy sorrows, as really as in thy joys. He lays low, and he builds up. Hold thy peace, and let thyself be guided by the hand of God; suffer in patience, and walk on in strong faith. Desire of God only one thing—that thou mayst spend thy life for his sake in true obedience and subjection. The way in which our blessed Savior trod was not one of softness and sweetness."—MOLINOS.

SONG OF DEATH.

ANONYMOUS.

Shrink not, O human spirit;
The everlasting arm is strong to save:
Look up, look up, frail nature; put thy trust
In Him who went down mourning to the dust,
And overcame the grave.
Quickly goes down the sun;
Life's work is almost done;
Fruitless endeavor, hope deferred, and strife;
One little struggle more,
One pang, and then is o'er
All the long, mournful weariness of life.
Kind friends, 'tis almost past;
Come now, and look your last;
Sweet children, gather near,
And his last blessing hear;
See how he loved you who departeth now;
And with thy trembling step and pallid brow,
O most belovéd one,
Whose breast he leaned upon,
Come, faithful unto death,
Receive his parting breath;
The fluttering spirit panteth to be free.
Hold him not back who speeds to victory.
The bonds are riven, the struggling soul is free.

Hail, hail, enfranchised spirit,
Thou that the wine press of the field hast trod;
On, blest immortal, on through boundless space,
And stand with thy Redeemer face to face,
And stand before thy God.
Life's weary work is o'er;
Thou art of earth no more;
No more art trammelled by th' oppressive clay,
But tread'st with wingéd ease
The high acclivities
Of truths sublime, up heaven's crystalline way.
Here no bootless guest;
The city's name is Rest;
Here shall no fear appall;
Here love is all in all;
Here shalt thou win thy ardent soul's desire,
Here clothe thee in thy beautiful attire.
Lift, lift thy wondering eyes;
Yonder is paradise;
And this fair, shining band
Are spirits of thy land;
And these that throng to meet thee are thy kin,
Who have awaited thee redeemed from sin.
The city's gates unfold: enter, O, enter in.

NO MORE.

Mrs. Hemans.

No more! a harpstring's deep, sad, breaking tone,
A last, low summer breeze, a far-off knell,
A dying echo of rich music gone,
Breathe through those words,—those murmurs of farewell,—
No more!

To dwell in peace with home affections bound,
To know the sweetness of a mother's voice,
To feel the spirit of her love around,
And in the blessing of her age rejoice,—
No more!

A dirge-like sound!—to greet the early friend
Unto the hearth, his place of many days;
In the glad song with kindred lips to blend,
Or join the household laughter by the blaze,—
No more!

Through woods that shadowed our first years to rove,
With all our native music in the air;
To watch the sunset with the eyes we love,
And turn and meet our own heart's answer there,—
No more!

Words of despair!—yet earth's, all earth's the woe
Their passion breathes,—the desolately deep!
That sound in heaven,—O, image, then, the flow
Of gladness in its tones!—to part, to weep,—
No more!

To watch in dying hope affection's wane,
To see the beautiful from life depart,
To wear impatiently a secret chain,
To waste the untold riches of the heart,—
No more!

Through long, long years to seek, to strive, to yearn
For human love, and never quench that thirst;
To pour the soul out, winning no return,
O'er fragile idols, by delusion nursed,—
No more!

On things that fail us, reed by reed, to lean;
To mourn the changed, the far away, the dead;
To send our searching spirits through th' unseen,
Intensely questioning for treasures fled,—
No more!

Words of triumphant music! bear we on
The weight of life, the chain, th' ungenial air;
Their deathless meaning, when our tasks are done,
To learn in joy;—to struggle, to despair,—
No more!

CROSSING THE DARK RIVER.

REV. E. MONRO.

It was a silent evening, and the sunset glowed over the distant hill. The faint stars came out one by one in the deep-blue sky, and they shed a pale light on the broad sheet of water, which flowed slowly and heavily on, of the Dark River. On the bank stood the family of Adeodatus, and I saw him among them. My attention was drawn towards them with increasing interest. I saw he was pale, deadly pale, but calm — calm as the still sunset on the hill; his eye was blue as a summer sky at midday, and his brow was solemn, thoughtful, and sad. His family were weeping around him, and I doubted not that he was about to cross the stream. I heard but few sounds; the words, "O Adeodatus! our dear Adeodatus!" sighed along the water's edge. But his gentle and quiet face seemed to hush them all. I was surprised beyond measure at the composure with which he came so close to the water at which he had so trembled at the distance. But I looked to the silver thread, and saw it was brilliant even to dazzling me.

"My mother, my mother!" said the youth, "I shall soon enter into the dark waters; but I feel calm; the silver thread is bound close around me, and it seems as if it would draw me on to the other side. Weep not for me, my mother, weep not for Adeodatus; but while you sojourn a while longer in the wilderness, think of the day when you must all cross the water. I fear it not; I know that He whom I have ever loved, though so weakly, will bear me safe through. Farewell, my family! my beloved family, farewell!" And as he spoke, his last accents were choked by the rising wave into which he had glided. All their eyes were fixed in the track of the water where their beloved had entered. But they saw no sign of his form; all they saw was the silver cord beneath the water, shining with crystal light, so as to light up the Dark River itself with its glory. They fixed their eyes on the other side, but they could not see across. The deep shadows hung there; and though some fancied they saw a light and a form on the side opposite where Adeodatus had entered, it was an indistinct fancy. He had passed away, and they saw him no more.

CHRISTIANS BY THE RIVER OF DEATH.

MRS. E. H. EVANS.

THERE came a little child, with sunny hair,
　All fearless to the brink of death's dark river,
And with a sweet confiding in the care
　Of Him who is of life the joy and giver;
And as upon the waves she left our sight,
We heard her say, "My Savior makes them bright."

Next came a youth, with bearing most serene,
  Nor turned a single backward look of sadness;
But as he left each gay and flowery scene,
  Smiling declared, "My soul is filled with gladness;
What earth deems bright forever I resign,
Joyful but this to know, that Christ is mine."

An aged mourner, trembling, tottered by,
  And paused a moment by the swelling river,
Then glided on, beneath the shadowy sky,
  Singing, "Christ Jesus is my strength forever.
Upon his arm my feeble soul I lean —
My glance meets his without a cloud between."

And scarce her last triumphant note had died,
  Ere hastened on a man of wealth and learning,
Who cast at once his bright renown aside,
  These only words unto his friends returning:
"Christ for my wisdom thankfully I own,
And as a little child I seek his throne."

Then saw I this — that whether guileless child,
  Or youth, or age, or genius, won salvation,
Each, *self-renouncing*, came; on each God smiled —
  Each found the love of Christ rich compensation
For loss of friends, earth's pleasures, and renown —
Each entered heaven, and "by his side sat down."

THE PILGRIM SAFELY ON THE OTHER SIDE OF THE DARK RIVER.

JOHN BUNYAN.

Now, upon the bank of the river, on the other side, they saw the two Shining Men again, who there waited for them. Wherefore, being come out of the river, they saluted them, saying, "We are ministering spirits, sent forth to minister for those that shall be heirs of salvation." . . . There, said they, is "the Mount Zion, the heavenly Jerusalem, the innumerable company of angels, and the spirits of just men made perfect." You are going now, said they, to the paradise of God, wherein you shall see the tree of life, and eat of the never-fading fruits thereof; and, when you come there, you shall have white robes given you, and your walk and talk shall be every day with the King, even all the days of eternity. There you shall not see again such things as you saw when you were in the lower region upon the earth, to wit, sorrow, sickness, affliction, and death, "for the former things are passed away." You are going now to Abraham, to Isaac, and to Jacob, and to the prophets, men that God hath taken away from the evil to come, and that are now "resting upon their beds, each one walking in his righteousness." . . . You must there receive the comfort of all your toil, and have joy for all your sorrow; you must reap what you have sown, even the fruit of all your prayers, and tears, and sufferings for the King by the way. In that place you must wear crowns of gold, and enjoy the perpetual sight and vision of the Holy One, for there "you shall see him as he is." There, also, you shall serve him continually with praise, with shouting, and thanksgiving, whom you desired to serve in the world, though with much difficulty, because of the infirmity of your flesh. There your eyes shall be delighted with seeing, and your ears with hearing, the pleasant voice of the Mighty One. There you shall enjoy your friends again that are gone thither before you; and there you shall with joy receive every one that follows into the holy place after you. There, also, you shall be clothed with glory and majesty, and put into an equipage fit to ride out with the King of Glory. When he shall come with sound of trumpet in the clouds, as upon the wings of the wind, you shall come with him; and, when he shall sit upon the throne of judgment, you shall sit by him: yea, and when he shall pass sentence upon all the workers of iniquity, let them be angels or men, you shall have a voice in that judgment, because they were his and your enemies. Also, when he shall again return to the city, you shall go, too, with sound of trumpet, and be ever with him.

THE GRAVE.

WASHINGTON IRVING.

THE sorrow for the dead is the only sorrow from which we refuse to be divorced. Every other wound we seek to heal, every other affliction to forget; but this wound we consider it a duty to keep open, this affliction we cherish and brood over in solitude. Where is the mother who would willingly forget the infant that has perished like a blossom from her arms, though every recollection is a pang? Where is the child that would willingly forget a tender parent, though to remember be but to lament? Who ever, in the hour of agony, would forget the friend over whom he mourns?

No, the love which survives the tomb is one of the noblest attributes of the soul. If it has its woes, it has likewise its delights; and when the overwhelming burst of grief is calmed into the gentle tear of recollection, when the sudden anguish and the convulsive agony over the present ruins of all that we most loved is softened away into pensive meditation on all that it was in the days of its loveliness, who would root out such a sorrow from the heart? Though it may sometimes throw a passing cloud over the bright hour of gayety, or spread a deeper sadness over the hour of gloom, yet who would exchange it even for the song of pleasure or the burst of revelry? No, there is a voice from the tomb sweeter than song. There is a remembrance of the dead to which we turn even from the charms of the living. O, the grave! It buries every error, covers every defect, extinguishes every resentment. From its peaceful bosom spring none but fond regrets and tender recollections. Who can look down upon the grave — even of an enemy — and not feel a compunctious throb, that he should have warred with the poor handful of earth that lies mouldering before him? But the grave of those we loved — what a place for meditation! There it is that we call up, in long review, the whole history of virtue and gentleness, and the thousand endearments lavished upon us almost unheeded, in the daily intercourse of intimacy; there it is that we dwell upon the tenderness, the solemn, awful tenderness of the parting scene; the bed of death, with all its stifled griefs, its noiseless attendance, its mute, watchful assiduities; the last testimonies of expiring love; the feeble, fluttering, thrilling — O, how thrilling! — pressure of the hand; the last fond look of the glazing eye turning upon us even from the threshold of existence; the faint, faltering accents struggling in death to give one more assurance of affection.

Ay, go to the grave of buried love, and meditate. There settle the account with thy conscience for every past benefit unrequited, every past endearment unregarded, of that departed being who can never, never, never return to be soothed by thy contrition. If thou art a child, and hast ever added a sorrow to the soul, or a furrow to the silvered brow, of an affectionate parent; if thou art a husband, and hast ever caused the fond bosom, that ventured its whole happiness in thy arms, to doubt one moment of thy kindness or thy truth; if thou art a friend, and hast ever wronged, in thought, or word, or deed, the spirit that generously confided in thee; if thou hast given one unmerited pang to that true heart which now lies cold and still beneath thy feet, — then be sure that every unkind look, every ungracious word, every ungentle action, will come thronging back upon thy memory, and knocking dolefully at thy soul; then be sure that thou wilt lie down sorrowing and repentant on the grave, and utter the unheard groan, and pour the unavailing tear — more deep, more bitter, because unheard and unavailing.

Then weave thy chaplet of flowers, and strew the beauties of nature about the grave; console thy broken spirit, if thou canst, with these tender, yet futile tributes of regret; but take warning by the bitterness of this thy contrite affliction over the dead, and henceforth be more faithful and affectionate in the discharge of thy duties to the living.

FAREWELL OF THE SOUL TO THE BODY.

MRS. SIGOURNEY.

COMPANION dear, the hour draws nigh,
The sentence speeds — *to die, to die.*
So long in mystic union held,
So close with strong embrace compelled,
How canst thou bear the dread decree
That strikes thy clasping nerves from me?
To Him who, on this mortal shore,
The same encircling vestment wore,
To him I look, to him I bend,
To him thy shuddering frame commend.
If I have ever caused thee pain,
The throbbing breast, the burning brain,
With cares and vigils turned thee pale,
And scorned thee when thy strength did fail,
Forgive, forgive! thy task doth cease,
Friend! lover! let us part in peace.
That thou didst sometimes check my force,
Or, trifling, stay mine upward course,
Or lure from heaven my wavering trust,
Or bow my drooping wing to dust,
I blame thee not; the strife is done;
I knew thou wert the weaker one,
The vase of earth, the trembling clod,
Constrained to hold the breath of God.

Well hast thou in my service wrought;
Thy brow hath mirrored forth my thought;
To wear my smile thy lip hath glowed,
Thy tear, to speak my sorrows, flowed;
Thine ear hath borne me rich supplies
Of sweetly-varied melodies;
Thy hands my prompted deeds have done,
Thy feet upon my errands run.
Yes, thou hast marked my bidding well,
Faithful and true! farewell, farewell.
Go to thy rest. A quiet bed
Meek Mother Earth with flowers shall spread,
Where I no more thy sleep may break
With fevered dream, nor rudely wake
Thy wearied eye.
O, quit thy hold,
For thou art faint, and chill, and cold,
And long thy gasp and groan of pain
Have bound me pitying in thy chain,
Though angels urge me hence to soar,
Where I shall share thine ills no more.
Yet we shall meet. To soothe thy pain,
Remember, we shall meet again.
Quell with this hope the victor's sting,
And keep it as a signet ring,
When the dire worm shall pierce thy breast,
And nought but ashes mark thy rest;
When stars shall fall, and skies grow dark,
And proud suns quench their glowworm spark,
Keep thou that hope, to light thy gloom,
Till the last trumpet rends the tomb.

Then shalt thou glorious rise, and fair,
Nor spot, nor stain, nor wrinkle bear,
And I, with hovering wing elate,
The bursting of thy bonds shall wait,
And breathe the welcome of the sky—
"No more to part, no more to die,
Co-heir of immortality."

FINAL REUNION OF THE SOUL AND BODY.

FLAVEL.

CHRIST'S body was raised from the dead to be glorified and crowned with honor. O, it was a joyful day to him; and so will the resurrection of the saints be to them the day of the gladness of their hearts. It will be said to them in that morning, "Awake and sing, ye that dwell in the dust." (Is. xxvi. 19.) O, how comfortable will be the meeting between the glorified soul and its new-raised body! For even glorified souls in heaven have such a desire of reunion. We are all sensible of the soul's affection to the body now, its sympathy with it, and unwillingness to be separated from it. It is said to be "at home in the body." (2 Cor. v. 6.) This inclination remains in heaven; it reckons not itself completely happy till its older, dear companion and partner be with it. Now, when this inclination to its own body, its longings after it, are gratified with the sight and enjoyment of it again, what a joyful meeting will this be! As the body shall be raised with all the improvements and endowments imaginable which may render it every way desirable, so the soul comes down immediately from God out of heaven, shining in its holiness and glory. And thus it reënters its body, and animates it again.

The chief joy of this meeting consists in *the end* for which the glorified soul comes down to quicken and repossess it, namely, to meet the Lord, and ever to be with the Lord; to receive a full reward for all the labors and services it performed for God in this world. This must make that day a day of triumph and exaltation. It comes out of the grave, as Joseph out of prison, to be advanced to the highest honor. O, do but imagine with what an ecstasy of joy the soul will thus resume its own body, and say, as it were, unto it, Come away, my dear, my ancient friend, who servedst and sufferedst with me in the world; come along with me to meet the Lord, in whose presence I have been ever since I parted with thee. Now, thy bountiful Lord hath remembered thee also, and the day of thy glorification is come. Surely it will be a joyful meeting. What a joy is it for dear friends to meet after a long separation! How they usually give demonstrations of their love and delight in each other by embraces, kisses, and tears! And frame to yourselves the idea of perfect health, when a sprightly vivacity runs through every part, and the spirits, as it were, overflow as we go about any business, especially such as the business of that day will be — to receive a crown and a kingdom. Do but imagine what a bright morning this will be, and how the pains and agonies, cold sweats and bitter groans, at parting will be recompensed by the joy of such a meeting!

HOPE FOR THE MOURNER.

BERNARD BARTON.

"But it shall come to pass, that at evening time it shall be light."
ZECH. xiv. 7.

WE journey through a vale of tears,
By many a cloud o'ercast,
And worldly cares and worldly fears
Go with us to the last.
Not to the last! THY WORD hath said,
Could we but read aright,
Poor pilgrim, lift in hope thy head;
At eve there shall be light.

Though earth-born shadows *now* may shroud
Thy thorny path a while,
God's blessed word can part each cloud,
And bid the sunshine smile.
Only BELIEVE, in living faith,
His love and power divine,
And ere thy sun shall set in death,
His light shall round thee shine.

When tempest clouds are dark on high,
  His bow of love and peace
Shines sweetly in the vaulted sky,
  Betokening storms shall cease.
Hold on thy way, with hope unchilled,
  By faith, and not by sight,
And thou shalt own His word fulfilled —
  At eve it shall be light.

IMMORTALITY.

G. Moore.

Morality and religion are based upon immortality; and not only so, but the emotions proper to moral and religious conduct necessarily indicate deathlessness. In short, we cannot entertain a notion of right and wrong without believing in a future state, or a life in which good or evil dispositions find their results. We are bound to right conduct, because the laws of Heaven are the laws of eternity, and we cannot escape the judgment *already* against us if we neglect our salvation. If nominal death, the death of the body, were the end of man's being, he might dismiss the claims of conscience from his soul; he would then have nothing to mind, nothing to concern himself about, but to take his ease as long as it lasted, and to seize upon the accommodations of this world of promise and provision to the best of his ability. . . . Those who do not look forward to a life beyond the grave really act on this unaccountable principle—"Let us eat and drink, for to-morrow we die." And they would be quite justified in so doing if something did not say within them, You cannot die—your God has to do with you forever.

. . . .

The immortality of the soul was implied in all the commandments of God under the Mosaic economy, and in the history of the patriarchs, and in all the trials of men's spirits from the beginning, because there was no sufficient end to be answered by the divine permission and providence as regarded man, unless in sustaining him in the hope of a future and enlarged existence. Hence the great cloud of witnesses adduced by Paul (Heb. xi.) as having acted under the power of faith with respect to the better resurrection, believing as they did in God as the Rewarder of his worshippers. And the translation of Enoch and of Elijah was the visible regeneration of the body itself under the act of the Almighty's will, by which man was fitted in a moment to exchange earth for heaven, as a spiritual being accommodated to a physical universe by a mediate body, capable of change according to the demands of the inhabiting spirit and the place in which it was required to dwell. There was always sufficient evidence on earth to induce the hope of another life, and plain facts asserted, to all who could credit honest testimony, the reasonableness of looking beyond this world for the fruition of a soul set on finding its Maker. The reasonableness of such a belief may be shown not only by reference to the evidences which revelation bears in itself, but also from the natural constitution of things, and from the unavoidable inferences of reason concerning the Creator's purpose, as evinced in the existence of mind and matter.

1st. Human immortality may be inferred, because a mind that is constituted to look forward to futurity with religious hope, and for the satisfaction of rational desire, cannot have answered the purpose for which it was created without the fulfilment of that hope and that desire. He who satisfies the desire of every living thing has not yet satisfied this desire. This argument, however, can have no weight but with those who experience the expressed state of mind. Those who are in the pitiable condition of being without this hope and this desire must be living without any consciousness of divine existence, and they need to be roused into spiritual vitality and vigilance before they can listen to arguments for eternal life. This is the work of God, and he is engaged in it by constraining men to reason from their experience, and their hopes, and their fears; for even doubt is an argument for immortality, since it implies the question of a mind that cannot rest in the expectation of nothingness, but believes only in an ever-coming to-morrow.

2d. If there be no future or continued existence, then the Maker of man has made him capable and desirous of learning more of his wisdom from his works, and yet has left him without any code of laws to govern his moral being, or any instruction sufficient to guide his inquiries concerning his future destiny; for moral laws are not binding on creatures destined to perish, and that doctrine is only deceptive which points to the light of heaven, and then leaves the soul to be quenched in everlasting darkness.

3d. If God has not left man without revelation, then man is immortal, because the only intelligence which he has received with any indication of its being revealed from God, is that which informs him of eternal safety as a reward, and eternal damage as a punishment, as the necessary consequence from the essential order of moral government.

4th. As what we learn concerning our Maker, from his works and his word, begets in all devout minds a happy reliance upon him and an adoring love, because of the cumulative proofs thus afforded of his benevolence and wisdom, and as this reliance and this love are in relation to a being who cannot cease to be adorable, there would be an incongruity of God's own making between the power to adore and the object of adoration, if man were not constituted, when actuated by indwelling truth, with a ceaseless capacity of worshipping and loving his Creator. But to suppose incongruity in God is to deny him.

5th. Without immortality, man would be a total contradiction to every idea of Deity ; and all earthly mental existence would be useless, because, although it seems to serve the purpose of manifesting God, it only serves, in fact, to excite hopes to end in disappointment, and to afford a taste of life which yet conveys to the spirit only death. The insect at the fountain may sip and sustain its powers, to fulfil the purposes of its little being ; but man must drink destruction at the source and streams of life, since his eagerness for intelligence and enjoyment leads only to his being lost amid the flood that flows from beneath the throne of God, unless he be immortal.

These arguments are mutually resolvable, the one into the other, and, after all, merely express an intuitive conviction that, because we are what we are, we must be something greater hereafter, and that we must continue to exist, since we cannot suppose our present state to be other than as a stage in our progress towards the full purpose of our existence.

If we do not believe in our future being, we must believe in something still more difficult to apprehend, for to expect continued life is according to our habit and our sense of probability ; but not to believe this, we must believe in annihilation ; but this we cannot, because we find no ground on which to proceed to such a conclusion, since there is no instance of such an event in all our knowledge, and therefore there can be no possibility of our supposing the Omnipotent engaged in blotting out his own work. . . . The preceding are the reasons which determine my own convictions, and they appear to me most consonant with the doctrines of the Bible and with man's moral consciousness. In short, I believe the soul is immortal, merely because it is a soul ; but without revelation there could not be a sufficient reason for a man's believing in immortality, since without that he would not have known enough of himself. What the heathen philosophers wanted in order to satisfy them, or at least to impart to them a hope full of immortality, was a true knowledge of God and of man. A mythology without an omnipotent Deity is a system without a sun — there is no cause of light or life in it — there is no being as the source and centre of existence, no mind interested in all other minds, no unity in intelligence, no bond of reason, no parent of spirits to whom they might come to dissipate their doubts. What was needed was a *Logos* to demonstrate that the Divinity was not a multitude of conflicting attributes, which men had imagined and adored as distinct deities, but that God was one, who, reconciling all things to himself, came forth to show himself as the Father of our spirits. When God was seen as love manifest in humanity, man was visibly immortal. It is in vain to reason of life everlasting without a demonstration of its cause, and that was never seen, except in as far as the Almighty made himself known as the immediate Friend of man. In the book of God we thus behold him. . . .

There is much said by religious writers concerning the difference between a natural or necessary immortality and a derived immortality. Let us understand our own words. What God wills, that is nature; what he does, that is necessary ; and he does what he wills. If, then, he wills that man should be immortal, man's immortality is natural and necessary. All that the creature possesses is, of course, by gift. God has immortality, but he has it to bestow : "the gift of God is eternal life by Jesus Christ."

"But is now made manifest by the appearing of our Savior Jesus Christ, who hath abolished death, and hath brought life and immortality to light through the gospel." — 1 TIMOTHY i.

"For this corruptible must put on incorruption, and this mortal *must* put on immortality. So when this corruptible shall have put on incorruption, and this mortal shall have put on immortality, then shall be brought to pass the saying that is written, Death is swallowed up in victory." — 1 CORINTHIANS xv.

INTIMATIONS OF IMMORTALITY.

R. H. Dana.

O, listen, man!
A voice within us speaks the startling word,
"Man, thou shalt never die!" Celestial voices
Hymn it around our souls; according harps,
By angel fingers touched when the mild stars
Of morning sang together, sound forth still
The song of our great immortality;
Thick-clustering orbs, and this our fair domain,
The tall, dark mountains, and the deep-toned seas,
Join in this solemn, universal song.
O, listen ye, our spirits; drink it in
From all the air. 'Tis in the gentle moonlight;
'Tis floating in day's setting glories; night,
Wrapped in her sable robe, with silent step
Comes to our bed, and breathes it in our ears;
Night and the dawn, bright day and thoughtful eve,
All time, all bounds, the limitless expanse,
As one vast, mystic instrument, are touched
By an unseen, living hand, and conscious chords
Quiver with joy in this great jubilee:
The dying hear it, and, as sounds of earth
Grow dull and distant, wake their passing souls
To mingle in this heavenly harmony.

THE RESURRECTION.

REV. HENRY MELVILL.

HAD not Christ undertaken the suretyship of our race, there would never have come a time when the dead shall be raised. If there had been no interposition on behalf of the fallen, whatever had become of the souls of men, their bodies must have remained under the tyranny of death. The original curse was a curse of death on the whole man. And it cannot be argued that the curse of the body's death could allow, so long as unrepealed, the body's resurrection. So that we may lay it down as an undisputed truth, that Christ Jesus achieved man's resurrection. He was emphatically the Author of man's resurrection. Without Christ, and apart from that redemption of our nature which he wrought out by obedience and suffering, there would have been no resurrection. It is just because the eternal Son took our nature into union with his own, and endured therein the curse provoked by disobedience, that a time is yet to arrive when the buried generations shall throw off the dishonors of corruption. . . . And if you call to mind the statement of St. Paul, "Since by man came death, by man came also the resurrection of the dead," (1 Cor. xv. 21,) you will perceive that the resurrection came by Christ, in exactly the same manner as death had come by Adam.

Now, we know that death came by Adam as the representative of human nature; and we therefore infer that the resurrection came by Christ as the representative of human nature. Retaining always his divine personality, the second person of the Trinity took our nature into union with his own; and in all his obedience, and in all his suffering, occupied this nature in the character and with the properties of a head. When he obeyed, it was the nature, and not a human person, which obeyed. When he suffered, it was the nature, and not a human person, which suffered. So that, when he died, he died as our head; and when he rose, he arose also as our head. And thus, — keeping up the alleged parallel between Adam and Christ, — as every man dies because concerned in the disobedience of the one, so he rises because included in the ransom of the other. Human nature having been crucified, and buried, and raised in Jesus, all who partake of this nature partake of it in the state into which it has been brought by a Mediator — a state of rescue from the power of the grave, and not of a continuance in its dark dishonors. The nature had almost literally died in Adam, and this nature did as literally revive in Christ. Christ carried it through all its scenes of trial, and toil, and temptation, up to the closing scene of anguish and death; and then he went down with it to the chambers of its lonely slumbers; and there he brake into shivers the chain which bound it and kept it motionless; and he brought it triumphantly back, the mortal immortalized, the decaying imperishable; and "I am the resurrection" was then the proclamation to a wondering universe. . . . Christ is more than the efficient cause of the resurrection : he is the resurrection. The untold myriads of our lineage rose in the resurrection of the new Head of our race. Never, O, never would the sheeted relics of mankind have walked forth from the vaults and the churchyards; never from the valley and the mountain would there have started the millions who have fallen in the battle tug; never would the giant caverns of the unfathomed ocean have yielded up the multitudes who were swept from the earth when its wickedness grew desperate, or whom stranded navies have bequeathed to the guardianship of the deep; never would the dislocated and decomposed body have shaken off its dishonors, and stood out in strength and in symmetry, bone coming again to bone, and sinew binding them, and skin covering them, had not He who so occupied the nature that he could act for the race, descended, in his prowess and his purity, into the chambers of death, and scattering the seeds of a new existence throughout their far-spreading ranges, abandoned them to gloom and silence till a fixed and on-coming day, appointing that then the seeds should certainly germinate into a rich harvest of undying bodies, and the walls of the chambers, falling flat at the trumpet blast of judgment, disclose the swarming armies of the buried marching onward to the "great white throne." (Rev. xx. 11.) . . . "The resurrection and the life" — these are thy magnificent titles, Captain of our salvation! And, therefore, we commit to thee body and soul; for thou hast redeemed both, and thou wilt advance both to the noblest and most splendid of portions. Who quails and shrinks, scared by the despotism of death? Who fears the dashings of those cold, black waters which roll between us and the promised land? Men and brethren, grasp your own privileges. Men and brethren, Christ Jesus has "abolished death." Will ye, by your faithlessness, throw strength into the skeleton, and give back empire to the dethroned and destroyed? Yes, "the resurrection and the life" "abolished death." Ye must indeed die, and so far death remains undestroyed. But if the terrible be destroyed when it can no longer terrify, and if the injurious be destroyed when it can no longer injure; if the enemy be abolished when it does the work of a friend, and if the tyrant be abolished when performing the offices of a servant; if the repulsive be destroyed when we can welcome it, and if the odious be destroyed when we can embrace it; if the quicksand be abolished when we can walk it and sink not; if the fire be abolished when we can pass through it and be scorched not; if the poison be abolished if we can drink it and be hurt not, — then is death destroyed, then is death abolished, to all who believe on the resurrection and the life; and the noble prophecy is fulfilled, — bear witness, ye groups of the ransomed, bending down from your high citadel of triumph, — "O death, I will be thy plagues; O grave, I will be thy destruction." (Hos. xiii. 14.)

"I heard a voice from heaven" — O for the angel's tongue, that words so beautiful might have all their melodiousness — "saying unto me, Write, Blessed are the dead which die in the Lord from henceforth; yea, saith the Spirit, that they may rest from their labors, and their works do follow them." (Rev. xiv. 13.) It is yet but a little while and we shall be delivered from the burden and the conflict, and with all those who have preceded us in the righteous struggle, enjoy the deep raptures of a Mediator's presence. Then, reunited to the friends with whom we took sweet counsel upon earth, we shall recount our toil only to heighten our ecstasy; and call to mind the tug and the din of war only that, with a more bounding throb and a richer song, we may feel and celebrate the wonders of redemption. And when the morning of the first resurrection breaks on this long-disordered and groaning creation, shall the words, whose syllables mingle so often with the funeral knell that we are disposed to carve them on the cypress tree rather than on the palm, "I am the resurrection and the life," form the chorus of that noble anthem, which those for whom Christ "died, and rose, and revived," (Rom. xiv. 9,) shall chant as they march from judgment to glory.

THERE IS A LAND.

REV. A. C. COXE.

"And I said, O that I had wings like a dove! then would I fly away and be at rest." — PSALTER.

THERE is a land like Eden fair,
But more than Eden blest;
The wicked cease from troubling there,
The weary are at rest.

There is a land of calmest shore,
  Where ceaseless summers smile,
And winds, like angel whispers, pour
  Across the shining isle.

There is a land of purest mirth,
  Where healing waters glide;
And there the wearied child of earth
  Untroubled may abide.

There is a land where sorrow's sons,
  Like ocean's wrecks, are tossed;
But there revive those weeping ones,
  And life's dull sea is crossed.

There is a land where small and great
  Before the Lord appear;
The spoils of fortune, and of fate,
  Whom Heaven alone can cheer.

There is a land where star-like shine
  The pearls of Christ's renown;
And gems, long buried in the mine,
  Are jewels in his crown.

There is a land like Eden fair,
  But more than Eden blest;
O for a wing to waft me there,
  To fly, and be at rest!

THE DYING CHRISTIAN TO HIS SOUL.

POPE.

VITAL spark of heavenly flame,
Quit, O, quit this mortal frame:
Trembling, hoping, lingering, flying,
O, the pain, the bliss of dying!
Cease, fond nature, cease thy strife,
And let me languish into life.

Hark! they whisper: angels say,
Sister spirit, come away.
What is this absorbs me quite?
Steals my senses, shuts my sight,
Drowns my spirits, draws my breath?
Tell me, my soul, can this be death?

The world recedes — it disappears;
Heaven opens on my eyes; my ears
With sounds seraphic ring:
Lend, lend your wings; I mount, I fly.
O grave, where is thy victory?
O death, where is thy sting?

THE FINAL JUDGMENT.

JOHN HARRIS, D. D.

HE who "sees the end from the beginning" has imparted to man a subordinate prescience of the same comprehensive kind — has sketched on his mind an outline of the great system of providence, and filled him with presentiments of the principal events which are to attend the development of that system. The consequence is, that, wherever the Bible comes, it finds our nature preconfigured to many of its truths, waiting for an interpreter, and ready to respond to the truth of many a prediction, as a prophecy or an anticipation with which it had long been familiar in thought, and for which it only wanted divine authentication, and a name, in order to regard it as a solemn reality. Indeed, in this respect, the work of God only resembles his word; for as in his word he has often disclosed the infinite affluences of his mind by revealing, with all the simplicity of apparent unconsciousness, an eternal principle in a passing word, an infinite project in an incidental allusion, so, in the construction of the human mind, he has traced on it characters and imagery which can only be read by the light of eternity; thrown on it the unsteady shadows of objects which stand yet far distant on the plains of futurity. Of these preintimations we know of none more deeply inlaid in the mind than that of future retribution. That the ancient saints lived in the faith of it, we know; for the spirit of inspiration has recorded the very words in which, in the prospect of that day, they triumphed over their persecutors, and sang of the joy that would crown them in "the day of the Lord." And, relying on the uniformity and immutability of the human constitution, we may safely infer that ancient sinners anticipated it also. There were moments when they possessed the warning of its approach in the restless apprehensions of their own breasts; moments when the fires of that day seemed to rise up in the distant horizon, and to cast a lurid glare on the face of their startled and trembling consciences; when the mention of such a day would have fallen in with the smothered forebodings of their minds, would have aroused an inward monitor, which, however carefully laid to sleep, was ready to awake at the slightest summons, and to bear testimony in the cause of righteousness.

But, though the doctrine of a future judgment did not originate in the teaching of Christ,—though, from the earliest ages, mankind had variously received it,—yet the light they possessed, even the revealed light, did but just suffice dimly to show them the Judge enthroned in clouds, and surrounded with judgments; while, from his superiority to temptation, his greatness and perfection, they inferred that the Judge of all the earth would do right. But the person of the Judge, the pomp and process of the judgment, its most solemn circumstances and affecting results,—all this was comparatively unknown to them; and, in supplying the information, our Lord has greatly enlarged the original part of his teachings.

Christ, when speaking of the final judgment, seldom omitted to insist and enlarge on its *publicity*. He thus reminds us, that the end for which there is any judgment at all is best secured by having it held in the presence of all worlds, that piety may be most honored, sin most abashed, and the government of God vindicated and glorified, on the largest possible scale. In a few descriptive words, he fills the horizon with intelligent beings of all orders and characters. It will not be the judgment of a single individual, nor of a nation, but of a whole world of intelligent and accountable beings. It will not be an assize for sins of recent commission merely; sins committed thousands of years before will be reproduced and examined, with all their circumstances of aggravation, as if they had been only just committed. What a profound impression will that produce of the holy character of God, and of the infinite enormity of sin! When his people are crowned, he would not have one of their enemies absent; and when the ungodly are doomed, he would not have one of the righteous absent: he would have them now to forestall that day — to feel, by anticipation, that they are speaking with the universe for their audience, and acting in the great theatre of the judgment; and *then*, he would have them depart to their respective allotments, bearing away with them impressions of the hatefulness of sin, and the beauty of holiness, which shall remain uneffaced through all the scenes of eternity.

"The Son of man shall come in his glory, and before him shall be gathered all nations." "The Father judgeth no man, but hath committed all judgment to the

Son." He hath "authority to execute judgment also, *because he is the Son of man;*" in his superadded humanity consists the very reason of his appointment. If the Judge is to be seen on that day with our bodily eyes, and if realities are to triumph on that day over appearances, substances over shadows, then is it fit that no illusion should sit on the throne, — that He should occupy it who is, "without controversy, God manifest in the flesh." If it was right in God so to construct the plan of salvation that in all its workings it should be made to yield to believers, as it does, the largest possible measure of consolation and joy, then must it be right, also, that, in the person of their Judge, they should recognize their Redeemer. It will give an additional value to the crown of life, that it will be bestowed by the hand of Christ; that the very Being who died for them, who gave them the grace of repentance, and who awakened in them the hope of salvation, should come personally to realize their hopes, to collect them around him, to wipe away every tear, to receive the plaudits of the universe in their salvation; this will be the only ingredient their cup of bliss will require, and the last it can receive; having that, their joy will be full. And if it be right that his enemies should be vanquished, it seems fit that he should vanquish them; if it is proper that unbelievers should be condemned, there appears a peculiar propriety that, both for their greater conviction and his greater exaltation, the sentence of condemnation should be pronounced by him.

And O, what an enhancement of their doom will this single circumstance contain! If a person be conscious that he is chargeable with ingratitude, and with ingratitude beyond forgiveness, he would rather confront his greatest foe than the person he has thus injured. Were any other being than Christ to ascend the throne of judgment, or were he any other than he is, the confusion of the impenitent sinner at appearing in his presence would be less intolerable. But when he shall draw near, and be compelled to look on that injured goodness, his confusion will be complete. When he shall behold him invested in the robe of humanity, that single sight will flash on him the recollection of all that Jesus did in that nature to redeem him: the incarnation, the bloody sweat, the cross, the pierced side — all will rise to view, and penetrate him with an agonizing sense of his ingratitude and guilt. When he shall hear the voice of that injured Being, the voice which he had heard so often in the gospel, inviting, entreating, beseeching him in every tone of gracious solicitude, it will vibrate on his ear more dreadfully than the sound of the archangel's trump, which called him from the grave. When the impenitent are represented as calling on the mountains and rocks to fall on them, what is that which they seek to avoid? They ask to be hidden from the face of Him that sitteth upon the throne, and from the wrath of the Lamb. *The wrath of the Lamb!* Had it been the fury of the lion; had it been the wrath of a being who had only created them, given them a law, and left them to obey it or perish, — who had only been known to them as a being of rigorous and unbending justice, — then, however conscious of guilt, they might have attempted to lift up their hardened front in his presence. But it is the wrath of the Lamb ; of a Being who has always acted towards them with infinite tenderness and patience ; who became the Lamb of God, the great sacrificial Victim, suffering and dying to take away their guilt. This is the circumstance which will render his wrath so unendurable that they will ask no higher favor than to be sheltered from the sight of his face, and would take the weight of the incumbent earth as a blessed exchange.

THE DAY OF JUDGMENT.

Rev. H. H. Milman.

Even thus amid thy pride and luxury,
O earth, shall that last coming burst on thee,
  That secret coming of the Son of man,
When all the cherub-throning clouds shall shine,
Irradiate with his bright, advancing sign ;
  When that great Husbandman shall wave his fan,
Sweeping like chaff thy wealth and pomp away ;
Still to the noontide of that nightless day
  Shalt thou thy wonted dissolute course maintain.
Along the busy mart and crowded street,
The buyer and the seller still shall meet,
  And marriage feasts begin their jocund strain ;
Still to the pouring out the cup of woe,
Till earth, a drunkard, reeling to and fro,
And mountains molten by his burning feet,
And heaven his presence own, all red with furnace
    heat.

The hundred-gated cities then,
The towers and temples, named of men
Eternal, and the thrones of kings;
The gilded summer palaces,
The courtly bowers of love and ease,
Where still the bird of pleasure sings;
Ask ye the destiny of them?
Go, gaze on fallen Jerusalem!
Yea, mightier names are in the fatal roll;
'Gainst earth and heaven God's standard is unfurled;
The skies are shrivelled like a burning scroll,
And one vast common doom insepulchres the world.
O, who shall then survive,
O, who shall stand and live,
When all that hath been is no more;
When, for the round earth hung in air,
With all its constellations fair,
In the sky's azure canopy;
When, for the breathing earth and sparkling sea,
Is but a fiery deluge without shore,
Heaven along the abyss profound and dark,
A fiery deluge, and without an ark?

Lord of all power, when thou art there alone
On thy eternal fiery-wheeléd throne,
That, in its high meridian noon,
Needs not the perished sun nor moon;
When thou art there in thy presiding state,
Wide-sceptred Monarch o'er the realm of doom,
When from the sea depths, from earth's darkest womb,
The dead of all the ages round thee wait;

And when the tribes of wickedness are strewn
  Like forest leaves in the autumn of thine ire;
Faithful and true! thou still wilt save thine own!
  The saints shall dwell within th' unharming fire,
Each white robe spotless, blooming every palm.
  Even safe as we, by this still fountain's side,
  So shall the church, thy bright and mystic bride,
Sit on the stormy gulf a halcyon bird of calm.
Yes! 'mid yon angry and destroying signs,
O'er us the rainbow of thy mercy shines:
We hail, we bless the covenant of its beam,
Almighty to avenge, almightiest to redeem!

THE RECOGNITION OF FRIENDS IN HEAVEN.

REV. BENJAMIN DORR, D. D.

WE have all lived to see many of our dearest friends and acquaintances removed to the world of spirits; and oft as busy memory retraces the scenes of by-gone years, and calls up the well-remembered forms — "the voice, the hand, the smile" — of the loved and lost, — "not lost, but gone before," — it is natural for us to inquire whether we shall ever meet to know each other again, and whether those attachments which we now cherish will remain after death.

Did we aim at logical accuracy, we should consider separately these several propositions: first, whether the *souls* of the righteous, in their disembodied state, and immediately after death, will know each other; or, secondly, whether this recognition, if it occur at all, takes place only after the reunion of soul and body at the resurrection day; and, thirdly, whether, if such knowledge exist, the attachments which bind us here will be continued hereafter. These subjects are, strictly speaking, entirely separate and distinct, inasmuch as there may be knowledge without affection; and if it were admitted that saints in light know each other, and all love each other, yet it does not necessarily follow that the peculiar ties which bind us here will be perpetuated hereafter. In like manner, if it be proved that friends will recognize each other in their glorified *bodies*, it does not follow, as a consequence, that pure disembodied spirits will possess such a recognition. To be strictly accurate, therefore, each of these separate propositions ought to be distinctly proved. It would, however, be foreign to our present purpose, and would be neither interesting nor instructive to our readers, to enter into all the niceties of the argument. We are aware that objections may be urged against the spirits of the righteous knowing each other, which would not apply to such a recognition in their glorified bodies. But, without attempting to answer such cavils, we can only say, in the words of the Rev. John Newton, "How wonderful will the moment after death be! how we shall see without eyes, hear without ears, and praise without a tongue, we cannot at present conceive. We now use the word *intuition*—then we shall know the meaning of it. But we are assured that they who love and trust the Savior shall see him as he is, and be like him and with him." We shall, therefore, consider the whole subject as one and indivisible, and attempt to show that departed spirits, "whether in the body or out of the body," will know each other, and that the pure and holy affections of love and friendship, which subsist now, will subsist forever.

This doctrine appears to be perfectly consonant to reason; for unless it be true that the souls of the righteous possess this knowledge, their views of God's wisdom, and justice, and mercy, and truth, must necessarily be very imperfect in a future state. The veracity of Him "who cannot lie" seems to stand pledged to assure us that he has, agreeably to his promises, conferred a superior degree of glory on those whose sufferings for the truth, and whose faith and patience in this life, were most conspicuous. Surely it will give us more exalted views of the faithfulness and love of Jehovah, to know that he has bestowed the greatest rewards on those who were distinguished for the greatest virtues; that the faith of an Abraham, the meekness of a Moses, the patience of a Job, the zeal of a Paul, and the fidelity of that host of apostles, martyrs, and confessors, who suffered for the cause of Christ, "not accepting deliverance," have been rewarded with a greater measure of bliss and glory. But to know this, it seems necessary that we should know the persons thus distinguished. And if we are permitted to know any of the saints in light, we see no reason why we may not know them all.

Again: we may reasonably suppose that a considerable part of the happiness of the saints will arise from a retrospection of those trials and difficulties which they have mutually encountered, and through which God has so mercifully conducted them. It must certainly be a delightful employment, and well calculated to increase their gratitude and joy, for those who have travelled together through life, sharing in each other's cares and sorrows, enduring the same "fight of afflictions," and struggling against the same temptations, to retrace the scenes through which they have passed, and to contrast their former "light afflictions" with their present "eternal weight of glory." This, however, could not be, unless there were a mutual recognition of each other. It is, therefore, in accordance with the soundest principles of reason, to suppose that the Christian will recognize in heaven those whom he loved on earth, and that the endearments of friendship will there be renewed and perpetuated. . . . That the pious and faithful under the Old Testament indulged this hope, and derived comfort from it, may be fairly inferred from several circumstances connected with the right of sepulture. On no other principle than the belief of meeting and recognizing their friends after death can we account for the deep solicitude which many of them expressed to have their bodies deposited in the same burial-place with those whom they loved on earth. If we suppose that Abraham, Isaac, Jacob, and Joseph believed in the resurrection of the body, and the recognition and reunion of departed relatives, we have a sufficient reason for their being so desirous of reposing beside their nearest earthly connections. But if they entertained no such hope, — if they did not believe that their bodies should rise again from the grave, or, when risen, that they would not recognize each other, — then how can we account for that inimitably beautiful and pathetic charge of Jacob to his children just before his death? "I am to be gathered unto my people: bury me with my fathers in the cave that is in the field of Ephron the Hittite; in the cave that is in the field of Machpelah, which is before Mamre, in the land of Canaan, which Abraham bought with the field of Ephron the Hittite for a possession of a burying-place. There they buried Abraham and Sarah his wife; there they buried Isaac and Rebekah his wife; and there I buried Leah." * He wished to be buried by the side of his nearest kindred, his aged father and mother, and his beloved wife. Why, but that he hoped to rise with them, to know them again, and to enter with them into the mansions of glory? If not, — if there was to be no recognition, — then might he as well have been buried among strangers in Egypt, as insist on being carried all the way to Canaan, to be placed in the cave of Machpelah. The same promise was exacted by Joseph of his brethren, and doubtless for the same reason. . . .

It is the expression of David, on being told that his child was dead, "Wherefore should I fast? can I bring him back again? I shall go to him, but he shall not return to me." This is evidently spoken by the Psalmist as a ground of comfort; the thought of going where his child had gone consoled him under the present affliction. Yet it could have been no source of consolation to him, if he had not expected to meet

* Genesis, xlix. 29–31.

and recognize his child again. Had David said, on this occasion, "I too shall die; my soul shall go to the place of departed spirits, and my body shall be buried in the ground; but my child shall never come back again to earth," — this would have been a mere truism; it is no expression of hope or comfort. But when he says, *I shall go to him*, we understand him to say, "I shall *see* him again, I shall *know* him again, I shall *embrace* him again;" and we then understand how he was comforted under the afflictive bereavement. . . .

There are two passages in St. Paul's Epistles which seem to place this subject beyond all question. They prove, at least, "that St. Paul anticipated on the last day a personal knowledge of those on his part, and a personal reunion with them, with whom he had been connected in this life by the ties of pastoral offices and kind affection."* To the Colossians he expresses the anxious desire of being able, in the day of Christ, to "present every man perfect in Christ Jesus;" and to the Thessalonians he thus writes: "For what is our hope, or joy, or crown of rejoicing? Are not even ye in the presence of our Lord Jesus Christ at his coming? For ye are our glory and joy." Here this great apostle evidently anticipates with delight the time when he should meet these persons before the throne, and "present" them to the Lord Jesus, "as the seals" — to borrow the language of the pious Doddridge — "which God had been pleased to set to his labors, and as amiable friends in whose converse and love he hoped to be

* Mant's Happiness of the Blessed, p. 82

forever happy." On this latter text the learned Dr. Macknight thus beautifully remarks : " The manner in which the apostle speaks of the Thessalonians shows that he expected to know his converts at the day of judgment. If so, we may hope to know our relations and friends then. And as there is no reason to think that in the future life we shall lose those natural and social affections which constitute so great a part of our present enjoyment, may we not expect that these affections, purified from every thing animal and terrestrial, will be a source of our happiness in that life likewise? It must be remembered, however, that in the other world we shall love one another, not so much on account of the relation and friendship which formerly subsisted between us, as on account of the knowledge and virtue which we possess; for among rational beings, whose affections will all be suited to the high state of moral and intellectual perfection to which they shall be raised, the most endearing relations and warmest friendships will be those which are founded on excellence of character. What a powerful consideration this to excite us to cultivate in our relations and friends the noble and lasting qualities of knowledge and virtue, which will prove such a source of happiness to them, and to us, through the endless ages of eternity!" If St. Paul expected to know his converts at the day of judgment, may not every Christian minister indulge this hope? Can there be a higher, holier anticipation — always excepting the hope of enjoying the beatific presence of God, and our Savior, and the holy angels — than that of meeting those whom we may have been instrumental in reclaiming from sin to holiness, and rescuing from the bitter pains of eternal death, to exalt them to glory, honor, and immortality? . . . In heaven, the love of God and the love of our neighbor will be our highest duty, our highest privilege, our highest joy; and so we trust it will be in reference to those endearments which now constitute the chief charm of life: they will be purified, strengthened, and perpetuated.

"I count the hope no daydream of the mind,
No vision fair of transitory hue,
The souls of those whom once on earth we knew,
And loved and walked with in communion kind,
Departed hence, again in heaven to find.
Such hope to nature's sympathies is true;
And such we deem the holy word to view
Unfolds — an antidote for grief designed,
One drop from comfort's well. 'Tis thus we read
The book of life; but if we read amiss,
By God prepared fresh treasures shall succeed
To kinsmen, fellows, friends, a vast abyss
Of joy; nor aught the longing spirit need,
To fill its measure of unmingled bliss."

Bishop Mant.

HEAVEN.

Rev. H. Melvill.

"And there shall be no night there, and they need no candle, neither light of the sun; for the Lord God giveth them light; and they shall reign forever and ever." — Revelation xxii. 5.

"They need no candle;" nay, they need not even the "light of the sun." "The Lord God giveth them light:"

is not this to say that the Lord God giveth them himself? for remember what is affirmed by St. John — "This then is the message which we have heard of him, and declare unto you, that God is light, and in him is no darkness at all." And therefore God, in some ineffable way, is to communicate himself to the soul. There will probably be a communication of ideas; * God will substitute his ideas, great, noble, luminous, for our own, contracted, confused, obscure; and we shall become like him in our measure, though participating his knowledge. There will be a communication of excellences: God will so vividly impress his image upon us that we shall be holy even as he is holy. There will be a communication of happiness; God will cause us to be happy in the very way in which he is happy himself, making what constitutes his felicity to constitute ours, so that we shall be like him in the sources or springs of enjoyment. All this seems included in the saying that the Lord God is to give us light. And though we feel that we are but laboring to describe, by all this accumulation of expression, what must be experienced before it can be understood, we may yet hope that we have caught something of the grandeur of the thought, that God himself is to be to us, hereafter, what the sun in the firmament is to us here. We wish to give, if possible, something of definiteness to the thought, by observing what an enlargement it supposes of all the powers of our nature; for now it would consume us to be brought into intimate intercourse with God; we must have the sun, we must have the candle; our faculties are not adapted to the living

* Saurin.

in his presence, where there is no veil upon his lustres. Hence we have in the figurative sketch of the text, in the part which makes God the source of all illumination, as well as in that which asserts the presence of night, a representation of man as nobly elevated amongst orders of being, and of the sublimest knowledge as thrown open to his search. Man is elevated, for he has passed from the ordinances and institutions of an introductory state to the open vision and free communion of spirits who never sullied their immortality. The sublimest knowledge is made accessible ; for, with God for his sun, into what depths can he penetrate, and not find fresh truths? With God as his temple, along what aisle of the stupendous edifice can he pass, and not collect from every column and every arch majestic discoveries? Where can he stand, and not hear the pervading spirit of the sanctuary breathing out secrets which he had vainly striven to explore, and wonders which he had not dared to conjecture. And thus, if it be a blessed thing to know that hereafter, set free from all the trainings of an elementary dispensation, we shall take our place, in the beauty and might of our manhood, amongst the nobles of creation ; that, gifted with capacities, and privileged with opportunities for deriving from immediate contact with Deity acquaintance with all that is illustrious in the universe, we shall no longer need those means and agencies, whether of nature or grace, which, whilst they strengthen and inform, prove us not made perfect ; yea, if it be a blessed thing to know this, it is also a blessed thing to hear that there shall be no candle, no sun, in the heavenly Jerusalem. The substitution of

God himself for every present source of light is among the most energetic representations of a change which lifts man into dignity, and gives the heights and depths to his survey; and therefore, so far as the ripening of our powers is concerned, or the moral splendor of our heritage, or the freedom of our expiations, description has well nigh exhausted itself in the announcement of the evangelist, that the inhabitants of the new Jerusalem "need no candle, neither light of the sun; for the Lord God giveth them light."

"And the city had no need of the sun, neither of the moon to share in it; for the glory of God did lighten it, and the Lamb is the light thereof. And the nations of them which are saved shall walk in the light of it; and the kings of the earth do bring their glory and honor into it. And the gates of it shall not be shut at all by day, for there shall be no night there." — REVELATION.

O, TALK TO ME OF HEAVEN.

BOWLES.

O, TALK to me of heaven! I love
To hear about my home above;
For there doth many a loved one dwell
In light and joy ineffable.
O, tell me how they shine and sing,
While every harp rings echoing;
And every glad and tearless eye
Beams, like the bright sun, gloriously.

Tell me of that victorious palm,
  Each hand in glory beareth,
Tell me of that celestial calm,
  Each face in glory weareth.

O, happy, happy country, where
  There entereth not a sin ;
And death, who keeps his portals fair,
  May never once come in.
No grief can change their day to night ;
The darkness of that land is light ;
Sorrow and sighing God hath sent
Far thence to endless banishment ;
And never more may one dark tear
  Bedim their burning eyes ;
For every one they shed while here,
  In fearful agonies,
Glitters a bright and dazzling gem,
In their immortal diadem.

O, lovely, blooming country! there
Flourishes all that we deem fair ;
And though no fields nor forests green,
Nor bowery gardens, there are seen,
  Nor perfumes load the breeze,
Nor hears the ear material sound,
Yet joys at God's right hand are found,
  The archetypes of these.
There is the home, the land of birth
Of all we highest prize on earth ;
The storms that rack this world beneath
  Must there forever cease ;

The only air the blessed breathe
 Is purity and peace.

O, happy, happy land! in thee
Shines the unveiled Divinity,
Shedding through each adoring breast
A holy calm, a halcyon rest.
And those blest souls whom death did sever
Have met to mingle joys forever.
O, soon may heaven unclose to me;
O, may I soon that glory see;
And my faint, weary spirit stand
Within that happy, happy land.

THE HAPPINESS OF HEAVEN.

PRESIDENT TIMOTHY DWIGHT.

IN this world we are children, standing on the bank of a mighty river. Casting our eyes upward and downward, along the channel, we discern various windings of its current, and perceive that it is now visible, now obscure, and now entirely hidden from our view. But being far removed from the fountains whence it springs, and from the ocean into which it is emptied, we are unable to form any conception of the beauty, usefulness, or grandeur of its progress. Lost in perplexity and ignorance, we gaze, wonder, and despond.

In this situation a messenger from Heaven comes to our relief, with authentic information of its nature, its course, and its end, conducts us backward to the fountains, and leads us forward to the ocean.

This river is the earthly system of Providence: the Bible is the celestial messenger, and heaven is the ocean in which all preceding dispensations find their end. In that glorious world no revelation will be needed to illumine the thoughts of its inhabitants concerning the divine administrations. . . . Possessed of superior vision, the eye will, here, with a direct and undeceiving survey, trace from the beginning the glorious dispensations of its Creator towards the various inhabitants of his boundless empire; will see them rise from little fountains, and, enlarging by continual addition, become mighty rivers. . . .

Christ is the light of heaven, as well as of the present world. He has taught us that he will feed his followers, and lead them to living fountains of waters. He will furnish them with that knowledge which is the true food of the mind, and, to slake their thirst for improvement, will lead them to the fountains of eternal wisdom, from which they shall drink forever. The perfections and pleasures of the Uncreated Mind he will eternally unfold, and direct them, throughout all the ages of heaven, in the paths of truth, virtue, and enjoyment. The instructor will be their Savior. The disciples will be those whom he has redeemed from perdition with his own precious blood. Think what must be the instructions of such a Teacher! what the improvement of such disciples! . . .

The heavenly inhabitants will render to God supreme and unmingled reverence. He will appear in his proper character, infinitely great and majestic, but divested of all those terrors, amid which he has so often manifested himself in the present world. He will no longer have *his way in the whirlwind and in the storm*, nor be surrounded by a flame of devouring fire. These were manifestations made to sinners, and will never be repeated in the heavenly world. *That fear of the Lord which is wisdom*, that *fear of the Lord which is a fountain of life*, will rise spontaneously, and delightfully, in every mind, when it fixes its eye on the greatness and purity of JEHOVAH, at once infinitely awful and lovely; while the *fear*, which *bringeth into bondage*, will by *perfect love be cast out forever*.

The mysteries, which in this world have perplexed their views concerning the dispensations and character of God, will there be finished by a complete disclosure of their nature, tendencies, and ends. It will there be clearly discerned, that in every case God proposed, and accomplished, that which was fittest to be done; that which, in the possession of clear, unprejudiced, unerring views, their own minds pronounce to be worthy of the universal Ruler. This conviction will preclude every doubt, every fear, concerning his future dispensations. The perfection of the *past* will be admitted without a question, as complete evidence of the perfection of the *future*. The soul, therefore, will cheerfully yield itself with implicit confidence to the guidance and conduct of its Creator throughout the never-ending progress of duration.

. . . . .

Heaven is the world of friendship; of friendship

unmingled, ardent, and entire. The disinterested love of the gospel dwells here in every bosom. Selfishness, since the ejection of the fallen angels from these delightful regions, has been here unknown and unheard of, except in the melancholy tidings, which have reached the happy inhabitants, of its deplorable effects on our apostate world. Here, every individual in the strictest sense fulfils the second great command of the moral law, and literally loves his neighbor as himself. No private, separate interest is ever proposed. A common good is announced by the voice of God, so great, as to comprise all individual happiness; so arranged as to furnish every one his proper portion, the part which he is to fulfil, and the means by which he is to act in it with absolute efficacy; and so noble as to fix every eye, engross every heart, and summon every effort. It is a good involving not only all that can be acquired, but all that can be wished, all that can exist. This great truth is, also, admitted with perfect confidence by every celestial mind. Every individual completely realizes the import and the truth of that glorious declaration of Christ, the foundation of all pure and lasting good, whether personal or social: *It is more blessed to give than to receive.* Under its influence, all the hearts and hands, all the mighty faculties and unwearied efforts, of the heavenly inhabitants, are completely occupied in doing good. To what a mass must this good arise where the work is carried on by saints and angels, in the great field of heaven, throughout the endless ages of duration! . . .

This friendship will endure forever. No degeneracy will awaken alarm and distrust, no alienation chill the heart, no treachery pierce the soul with anguish. No parent will mourn over an apostate child, and no child over a profligate parent. No brothers, nor sisters, will be wrung with agony by the defection and corruption of those who, inexpressibly endeared to them in this world by the tender ties of nature, and the superior attachments of the gospel, have here walked with them side by side in the path of life, and have at length become their happy companions in the world of glory. Husbands and wives, also, here mutually and singularly beloved, will there be united, not indeed in their former earthly relation, but in a friendship far more delightful, and, wafted onward by the stream of ages without a sigh, without a fear, will become, in each other's eyes, more and more excellent, amiable, and endeared, forever.

. . . . .

To the eye of man the sun appears a pure light, a mass of unmingled glory. Were we to ascend with a continual flight towards this luminary, and could we, like the eagle, gaze directly on its lustre, we should in our progress behold its greatness continually enlarge, and its splendor become every moment more intense. As we rose through the heavens, we should see a little orb changing, gradually, into a great world; and as we advanced nearer and nearer, should behold it expanding every way, until all that was before us became a universe of excessive and immeasurable glory. Thus the heavenly inhabitant will, at the commencement of his happy existence, see the divine system filled with magnificence and splendor, and arrayed in glory and beauty; and as he advances onward through the successive periods of duration, will behold all things more and more luminous, transporting, and sunlike, forever.

HEAVEN.

BISHOP KEN.

THE saints in happy mansions rest,
Of all they can desire possessed ;
No misery, want, or care,
No death, no darkness there,
No troubles, storms, sighs, groans, or tears,
No injury, pain, sickness, fears.

There saints no disappointments meet ;
No vanities, the choice to cheat ;
Nothing that can defile ;
No hypocrite, no guile ;
No need of prayer, or what implies
Or absence or vacuities.

There no ill conscience gnaws the breast ;
No tempters holy souls infest ;
No curse, no weeds, no toil ;
No errors to embroil ;
No lustful thoughts can enter in,
Or possibility of sin.

Saints' bodies there the sun outvie,
Tempered to feel the joys on high:
Bright body and pure mind
In rapture unconfined,
Capacities expand, till fit
Deluge of Godhead to admit.

With God's own Son they reign co-heirs;
Each saint with him in glory shares:
Like Godhead, happy, pure,
Against all change secure,
In boundless joys they sabbatize,
Which love triune will eternize.

"WHAT MUST IT BE TO BE THERE!"

ANONYMOUS.

We speak of the realms of the blest,
  Of that country so bright and so fair,
And oft are its glories confessed;
  But what must it be to be there!

We speak of its pathways of gold,
  And its walls decked with jewels most rare,
Of its wonders and pleasures untold;
  But what must it be to be there!

We speak of its freedom from sin,
  From sorrow, temptation, and care,
From trials without and within;
  But what must it be to be there!

We speak of its service of love,
  Of the robes which the glorified wear,
Of the church of the first-born above;
  But what must it be to be there!

Then let us, 'midst pleasure and woe,
  Still for heaven our spirits prepare;
And shortly we also shall know
  And feel what it is to be there!

ETERNITY.

HERVEY.

O ETERNITY, eternity! how are our boldest, our strongest thoughts lost and overwhelmed in thee! Who can set landmarks to limit thy dimensions, or find plummets to fathom thy depths? *Arithmeticians* have figures to compute all the progressions of time; *astronomers* have instruments to calculate the distances of the planets; but what numbers can state, what lines can gauge, the lengths and breadths of eternity? "It is higher than heaven, what canst thou do? Deeper than hell, what canst thou know? The measure thereof is longer than the earth, broader than the sea."

Mysterious, mighty existence! a sum not to be lessened by the largest *deductions!* an extent not to be contracted by all possible *diminutions!* None can truly say, after the most prodigious waste of ages, "So much of eternity is gone;" for, when millions of centuries are elapsed, it is but just commencing; and when millions more have run their ample round, it will be no nearer ending. Yea, when ages numerous as the bloom of spring, increased by the herbage of summer, both augmented by the leaves of autumn, and all multiplied by the drops of rain which drown the winter, — when these, and ten thousand times ten thousand more, more than can be represented by any similitude, or imagined by any conception, — when all these are revolved and finished, eternity — vast, boundless, amazing eternity — will *only be beginning!*

THE SILENT LAND.

SALIS.

INTO the silent land —
Ah! who shall lead us thither?
Clouds in the evening sky more darkly gather
And shattered wrecks lie thicker on the strand.
Who leads us with a gentle hand
Thither, O, thither,
Into the silent land?

Into the silent land!
To you, ye boundless regions
Of all perfection! Tender morning visions
Of beauteous souls! The Future's pledge and band
Who in life's battle firm doth stand,
Shall bear Hope's tender blossoms
Into the silent land.

O land! O land
For all the broken-hearted!
The mildest herald by our fate allotted
Beckons, and with inverted torch doth stand
To lead us with a gentle hand
Into the land of the dear departed,
Into the silent land.

"There is a path which no fowl knoweth, and which the vulture's eye hath not seen: the lion's whelps have not trodden it, nor the fierce lion passed by it. But where shall wisdom be found? and where is the place of understanding? Man knoweth not the price thereof; neither is it found in the land of the living. The depth saith, It is not in me: and the sea saith, It is not with me. *Destruction* and *death* say, We have heard the fame thereof with our ears. God understandeth the way thereof, and he knoweth the place thereof: for he looketh to the ends of the earth, and seeth under the whole heaven." — JOB xxviii.

WEEP NO MORE.

MISS ROSCOE.

WEEP no more that the azure eye
Hath ceased to glisten,
That the wavy locks in the damp grave lie,
That the lip hath lost its crimson dye,
That you vainly listen
For the voice of witching melody.
Weep no more that each fleeting trace
This earth had given
Hath left forever the form and face,
That the soul hath run its mortal race,
And the joys of heaven
The changing woes of this world replace.
Weep no more, O, weep no more!
Wouldst thou restore
The colors that decked the worm before?
Wouldst thou its grovelling shape restore
For the lovelier hues,
The lighter wings, that heavenward soar?

"Son of man, behold, I take away from thee the desire of thine eyes with a stroke; yet neither shalt thou mourn nor weep, neither shall thy tears run down." — EZEK. xxiv.

"And God shall wipe away all tears from their eyes; and there shall be no more death, neither sorrow nor crying; neither shall there be any more pain; for the former things are passed away." — REV. xxi.

THE DYING BELIEVER TO HIS SOUL.

TOPLADY.

DEATHLESS principle, arise!
Soar, thou native of the skies!
Pearl of price by Jesus bought,
To his glorious likeness wrought,
Go to shine before his throne;
Deck his mediatorial crown.
Go his triumph to adorn;
Made for God, to God return.
Lo, he beckons from on high!
Fearless to his presence fly;
Thine the merit of his blood,
Thine the righteousness of God.
Angels, joyful to attend,
Hovering round thy pillows bend,
Wait to catch the signal given,
And escort thee safe to heaven.
Is thy earthly house, distressed,
Willing to retain her guest?
'Tis not thou, but she, must die.
Fly, celestial tenant, fly!
Burst thy shackles, drop thy clay,
Sweetly breathe thyself away;
Singing, to thy crown remove,
Swift of wings and fired with love.

Shudder not to pass the stream ;
Venture all thy care on Him —
Him whose dying love and power
Stilled its tossings, hushed its roar.
Safe is the expanded wave,
Gentle as a summer's eve ;
Not one object of his care
Ever suffered shipwreck there.
See the haven full in view !
Lovė divine shall bear thee through ;
Trust to that propitious gale ;
Weigh thy anchor, spread thy sail.
Saints in glory, perfect made,
Wait thy passage through the shade ;
Ardent for thy coming o'er,
See, they throng the blissful shore !
Mount, their transports to improve !
Join the longing choir above ;
Swiftly to their wish be given ;
Kindle higher joy in heaven.
Such the transports that arise
To the dying Christian's eyes ;
Such the glorious vista faith
Opens through the shades of death.

TO A DYING INFANT.

ANONYMOUS.

SLEEP, little baby, sleep!
  Not in thy cradle bed,
Not on thy mother's breast,
Henceforth shall be thy rest,
  But with the quiet dead.

Yes, with the quiet dead,
  Baby, thy rest shall be;
O, many a weary wight,
Weary of light and life,
  Would fain lie down with thee!

Flee, little tender nursling,
  Flee to thy grassy nest!
There the first flower shall blow;
The first pure flake of snow
  Shall light upon thy breast.

Peace! peace! The little bosom
  Labors with short'ning breath;
Peace! peace! That trem'lous sigh
Speaks his departure nigh;
  These are the damps of death.

I've seen thee in thy beauty,
  A thing all health and glee;

But never then wert thou
So beautiful as now,
  Baby, thou seem'st to me.

Thine upturned eyes glazed over,
  Like harebells wet with dew,
Already veiled and hid
By the enamelled lid,
  Their pupils darkly blue.

Thy little mouth half open,
  Thy soft lip quivering,
As if, like summer air
Rustling the rose leaves there,
  Thy soul were fluttering.

Mount up, immortal essence!
  Young spirit, haste, depart!
And is this death? Dread thing!
If such thy visiting,
  How beautiful thou art!

O, I could gaze forever
  Upon thy waxen face,
So passionless, so pure!
The little shrine was sure
  An angel's dwelling-place.

Thou weepest, childless mother;
  Ay, weep — 'twill ease thy heart.
He was thy first-born son,
Thy first, thine only one;
  'Tis hard from him to part; —

'Tis hard to lay thy darling
  Deep in the damp, cold earth—
His empty crib to see,
His silent nursery,
  Once gladsome with his mirth;—

To meet again in slumber
  His small mouth's rosy kiss,
Then, waking with a start,
By thine own throbbing heart
  His twining arms to miss;—

To feel, half conscious why,
  A dull, heart-sinking weight,
Till memory on thy soul
Flashes the painful whole,
  That thou art desolate;—

And then to lie and weep,
  And think, the livelong night,
Feeding thine own distress
With accurate greediness
  Of every past delight;—

Of all his winning ways,
  His pretty, playful smiles,
His joy at seeing thee,
His tricks, his mimicry,
  And all his little wiles;—

O, these are recollections
  Round mothers' hearts that cling,

That mingle with the tears
  With soft awakening!

Thou'lt say, " My first-born blessing,
  It almost broke my heart
When thou wert forced to go;
And yet for thee I know
  'Twas better to depart.

" God took thee in his mercy,
  A lamb untasked, untried;
He fought the fight for thee,
He won the victory,
  And thou art sanctified.

" I look around and see
  The evil ways of men;
And O, belovéd child,
I'm more than reconciled
  To thy departure then.

" The little arms that clasped me,
  The innocent lips that pressed,
Would they have been as pure
Till now as when of yore
  I lulled thee on my breast?

" Now, like a dewdrop shrined
  Within a crystal stone,
Thou'rt safe in heaven, my dove —
Safe with the Source of love,
  The everlasting One.

"And when the hour arrives
  From flesh that sets me free,
Thy spirit may await,
The first at heaven's gate
  To meet and welcome me."

HOW SHALL WE KNOW THEM?

MISS ROSCOE.

How shall we know them, — the infant race?
How will the mother her loved one trace?
Not by the glance of the sunny eye,
'T was but a gleam o'er mortality;
Not by her look as she sunk to rest,
A closing flower on her throbbing breast;
But by a feeling like that which burned
When her heart o'er the guileless stranger yearned,
By a thrill like that which, when first she smiled,
Came o'er her soul, shall she know her child.

COMFORT, COMFORT MY SWEET MOTHER.

ANONYMOUS.

"In heaven their angels do always behold the face of my Father."

SILENCE filled the court of Heaven,
Hushed were angel harp and tone,
As a little new-born spirit
Knelt before the eternal throne;
While his snow-white hands were lifted
Clasped as if in fervent prayer,
And his voice in low, sweet murmurs
Fell like music on the air;
Light from the full fount of glory
On his robe of whiteness glistened,
And the bright-winged seraphs round him
Bowed their radiant heads and listened.

"Lord, from thy world of glory here
My heart turns fondly to another,
O Lord, our God, the Comforter,
Comfort, comfort my sweet mother!
Many sorrows hast Thou sent her,
Meekly has she drained the cup,
And the jewels Thou hast lent her
Unrepining yielded up:
Comfort, comfort my sweet mother!

"Earth is growing lonely round her,
Friend and lover hast Thou taken;
Let her not, though clouds surround her,
Feel herself by Thee forsaken;

Let her think, when faint and weary,
We are waiting for her here;
Let each loss that makes earth dreary
Make the thought of Heaven more dear:
Comfort, comfort my sweet mother!

"Thou who, from the heavens descending,
Fears, and woes, and sufferings won,
Thou who, nature's laws suspending,
Gave the widow back her son,
Thou who at the grave of Lazarus
Wept with those who wept their dead,
Thou who once in mortal anguish
Bowed thine own immortal head,
Comfort, comfort my sweet mother!

"Saviour, thou in nature human
Knelt on earth a little child,—
Pillowed on the heart of woman,
Blessed Mary, undefiled.
Thou! who from the cross of suffering,
Marked thy mother's tearful face,
And bequeathed her to thy loved one,
Bidding him to fill thy place,
Comfort, comfort my sweet mother!"

The dove-like murmur died away
Upon the radiant air,
But yet the little suppliant knelt
With hands still clasped in prayer.
Still were his gently pleading eyes
Turned to the sapphire throne,
Till golden harp and angel voice

Rang out in mingled tone;
And as the silvery numbers swelled,
By seraph voices given,
High, clear, and sweet the anthem rolled
Through all the gates of Heaven.
"He chastens whom he loves," it said,
"As a Father his own son."
The infant cherub bowed his head:
"Thy will, O Lord! be done."

"Afflictions are the same to the soul as the plough to the fallow-ground, the pruning-knife to the vine, and the furnace to the gold." — JAY.

CONSOLING THOUGHTS FOR THE AFFLICTED CHRISTIAN.

RACHEL, LADY RUSSELL.

THE consideration of the other world is not only a very great, but, in my small judgment, the only support under the greatest of afflictions that can befall us here; the enlivening heat of those glories is sufficient to refresh us in our dark passage through the world. . . . . God will help us in believing; and though he suffers us to be cast down, will not cast those off who commit their cause to him. . . . . But who knows, says Solomon, what is good for a man in this life? all the days of his vain life? Yet there is an inseparable connection between God's wisdom and his will; so his work is perfect, for all his ways are judgment. . . . . While we are clothed with flesh, to the perfectest, some displeasure will attend a separation from things we love. This comfort, I think, I have in my affliction, that I can say, unless the law had been my delight, I should have perished in my trouble.

But we must wait for the day of consolation till this world passes away. God knows what is best; all his dispensations serve the end of his providences; and they are ever beautiful, and must be good, and good to every one of us; if we can bear evidence to our own souls, that we are better for our afflictions. We may reasonably hope that our friends find that rest we yet hope for; and what better comfort can we desire in this valley of the shadow of death we are walking through? The rougher our path is, the more delightful and ravishing will the great change be to us.

BITTER SWEET.

REV. GEORGE HERBERT.

AH, my deare angrie Lord,
  Since thou dost love, yet strike;
Cast down, yet help afford;
  Sure I will do the like.

I will complain, yet praise;
  I will bewail, approve:
And all my soure-sweet dayes
  I will lament, and love.

ANGELS.

INSCRIBED TO THE MEMORY OF OUR DARLING "HATTIE," WHO WAS NUMBERED WITH THE ANGELS, MAY 13, 1857.

H. W. ROCKWELL.

WHENE'ER the balms of night my spirit cumber,
I hear the tread of angels without number,
Stealing on tiptoe through the gates of slumber.

Like the soft fires of morning newly-risen,
Around, on every side, their pinions glisten,
And there are voices unto which I listen;

Voices which strike upon my charmèd ear
Like the sweet music of some distant sphere,
As if a thousand flutes were warbling near.

And with them come sweet thoughts, — joys long since o'er,
And memories of those that went before,
Down to the dark and distant Evermore.

They who passed hence, — the gentle and the lovely,
Ebbing away from life so calm and slowly,
That death itself seemed beautiful and holy;

And 'mid them all, two little forms that stand,
With eyes bent earthward from that summer-land,
The fairest of that fair and glittering band.

Brightening upon my rapt, bewildered vision,
I see the footsteps of that countless legion,
Sliding, like golden fires, from Heaven's sweet region.

And in the air I hear their gentle voices,
Above the reach of Earth's discordant noises:
I hear them, — and my saddened heart rejoices.

Therefore, whene'er I feel life's load of pain,
It seems to me as if Heaven's golden chain
Grew, link by link, more beautiful again;

For could we fathom with unclouded eyes
The viewless mystery that 'round us lies,
Grief would appear but "blessings in disguise."

O breaking hearts! — whose nights are nights of weeping:
O weary eyes! — that close, but know no sleeping:
God hath vouchsafed to you his holy keeping.

He will not leave you utterly forsaken,
Though every comfort from your side be taken:
Nor will he break the reed, though bruised and shaken.

From out the waves of Death's dark-rolling river, —
Its gloomy plunge, its cold and icy shiver, —
His mighty ransom shall your soul deliver,

For He his angels charge of thee hath given;
And though by sorrow here thou mayst be riven,
There is a rest awaiting thee in heaven!

"He will swallow up death in victory, and the Lord God will wipe away all tears." — Isaiah xxv.

LETTER OF CONSOLATION TO AN AFFLICTED MOTHER.

Archibald Alexander, D. D.

I am afraid from what I have heard, and from the strain of your letter, that your grief, on account of the death of your beloved daughter, has been excessive; that you have yielded more than was good to despondency; and that you are in danger of sinking into a settled dejection. I know that your natural disposition exposes you to an extreme on this side, and that, unless you vigorously and resolutely oppose it, you will be likely to do yourself a serious, and perhaps a lasting injury. Grief, like all other natural passions, becomes sinful when indulged too far. It then involves always some want of confidence in God, some improper feeling in regard to his government and will. It partakes of the nature of that sorrow which worketh death. It wastes the spirits, debilitates the body, predisposes to various diseases, unfits for the discharge of common duties, destroys one's own peace, and adds to the unhappiness of friends. Somehow or other, we are not so much afraid of sin, when it approaches us through this channel. If we grow light and indulge a love of pleasure, conscience is soon roused; but we are ready to justify our sorrow, and refuse to make the effort which is necessary to check it. There is often a strong perverseness in the human mind in hugging its sorrows, as if they were valuable or sacred. But while the religion of Christ permits us to indulge our natural feelings, it strictly requires temperance here, as well as in other indulgences. It requires us to rejoice, to rejoice always, and to rejoice in tribulation. I feel for you under the sore bereavement which you have suffered; but the stroke, though severe, comes from the hand of a Father, who afflicts not willingly. Our children are more the property of God than of ourselves. He gave and he taketh away, and it is our duty to submit to his will in all things; for whatever he does is right and best for his own children.

"Is there no balm in Gilead; is there no physician there?"
JEREMIAH viii.

GOD'S WILL THE BEST.

ANONYMOUS.

WHATE'ER God does is fitly done,—
And all for wisest reasons;
By best of paths he leads me on,
And at the darkest seasons;
I find his grace
In every place;
And, conscious of his keeping,
I change to joy my weeping.

Whate'er God does is fitly done.
His cup, — shall I refuse it,
Because it is a bitter one?
He sees it best, — I choose it.
And He at last
Will make me rest
Where duty has no trials,
And needs no self-denials.

"The truly great and good, in affliction, bear a countenance more princely than they are wont; for it is the temper of the highest hearts, like the palm-tree, to strive most upwards when they are most burdened." — Sir Philip Sidney.

"Before an affliction is digested, consolation ever comes too soon; — and after it is digested, it comes too late: there is but a mark between these two, as fine almost as a hair, for a comforter to take aim at." — Sterne.

THOU HAST LEFT US.

ANONYMOUS.

Thou hast left us, and the life-tide
Flows with sadder pulses now,
And we miss thy well-known foot-fall,
And the smile upon thy brow.

Thou hast left us, — O the sadness
Dwelling in those simple words,
Striking out the light of gladness,
Muffling all the spirit-chords!

Thou hast left us; but in spirit
Walk we ever side by side,

And we hear thy low, sweet whisper
  At the dawn and even-tide.

Thou hast left us; but around us,
  Wafted on the wings of love,
Float the memories that bound us,
  And our soul's deep fountains move.

Thou hast left us; — Heaven seems nearer,
  That thy feet have trod its shore;
And the earth is darker, drearer,
  That we see thy face no more.

Thou hast left us; — dost thou miss us,
  In that far-off, happy land?
Soon death's icy lips will kiss us,
  And unite our broken band.

Thou hast left us; — sad and tearful,
  Mingling in earth's care and strife,
Bowed in spirit, trembling, fearful,
  Wait we for the higher life.

Thou hast left us; — Oh! wait for us
  On that ever-verdant shore, —
Thou hast crossed the tide before us,
  And we quail not at its roar.

Thou hast left us; — but for ever
  Pangs of parting may not be, —
Love's strong bands are sundered never,
  In the land beyond death's sea.

"The Lord upholdeth all that fall, and raiseth up all those that be bowed down." — PSALM cxlv.

THE REDEEMED IN GLORY.

REV. JAMES HAMILTON.

IF any of your friends have slept in Jesus, is it not blissful to know how they are engaged? You and they once journeyed together; but a sudden door opened, and your father or brother or child was snatched from your side; and ere you could follow, or even glance in, the door closed again. But the Lord has opened a crevice in the enclosing wall, and bids you look and see. See where they are, — see what they are doing. *You* are in great tribulation, — it is even your tribulation to be deprived of *them;* but they have come out of all tribulation. You often find it hard to reach the throne of grace, — hard to prevail with yourself to pray; they never quit the throne of God, but serve him day and night in his temple. It is only by faith that you can walk with Jesus; they see God, and follow the Lamb whithersoever he goeth. You suffer much from sickness and languor, and bodily discomfort, — our summers are too sultry, and our frosts too keen, — and you lose much time from infirmities of the flesh: they hunger no more, neither thirst any more; neither does the the sun light on them, nor any heat. Your heart is often like to break; between the unkindness of some, and the sufferings of others, you have tears to drink in great measure: God himself has wiped away all tears from *their* eyes. Your best powers and most blessed services are very brief. There is only one Sabbath in your week, and that is soon gone. *Their* palm never withers; their hallelujahs never cease; their congregation never breaks up; their Sabbaths know no end.

> "Je te salue, Ô Mort! Libérateur céleste,
> Tu ne m'apparais point sous cet aspect funeste
> Que t'a prêté longtemps l'epouvante ou l'erreur;
> Ton bras n'est point armé d'un glaive destructeur,
> Ton front n'est point cruel, ton œil n'est point perfide."

TRANSLATION.

"Hail Death, thou great deliverer! Thou dost not now appear to me in that dreary aspect thou hadst borrowed, so long, from error and fear. Thy hand is no more armed with a destructive sword, thy countenance is no more cruel, nor thine eye false." — LAMARTINE'S MEDITATIONS.

SONG OF THE REDEEMED SOUL IN HEAVEN.

ANONYMOUS.

I SHINE in the light of God,
His likeness stamps my brow;
Through the shadow of death my feet have trod,
And I reign in glory now;
No breaking heart is here,
No keen and thrilling pain,
No wasted cheek, where the frequent tear
Hath rolled and left its stain.

I have found the joys of heaven,
I am one of the angel band;
To my head a crown is given,
And a harp is in my hand.

I have learned the song they sing
  Whom Jesus hath made free,
And the glorious halls of heaven still ring
  With my new-born melody.

No sin, no grief, no pain,
  Safe in my happy home,
My fears all fled, my doubts all slain,
  My hour of triumph come,
O friends of my mortal years,
  The trusted and the true,
Ye 're walking still in the valley of tears,
  And I wait to welcome you.

Do I forget? O no!
  For memory's golden chain
Shall bind my heart to hearts below,
  Till they meet and touch again.
Each link is strong and bright,
  And Love's electric chain
Flows freely down, like a river of light,
  To the world from whence I came.

Do you mourn when another star
  Shines out from the glittering sky?
Do you weep when the voice of war
  And the rage of conflict die?
Then why should your tears roll down
  And your heart be sorely riven,
For another gem in the Saviour's crown,
  And another soul in heaven?

"Few mercies call for more thankfulness than a friend safe in heaven."
— HAMILTON.

CHRISTIANITY THE RELIGION OF SORROW.

Rev. J. J. Taylor.

Christianity, in the highest sense, is the religion of sorrow. It baptizes the heart with a holy sadness, and prepares it for the descent of the Spirit of God. Christ leads us on to perfection, as a man of sorrows and acquainted with grief. Gethsemane and Calvary are the scenes where he teaches us most effectually the necessity of life's struggles, and the secret of its consolations. All that concerns the interest of the present life we can learn for ourselves, and from those with whom we daily live. Science and human experience suffice for this. What we need is the higher discipline that will convert pain, and toil, and grief, and disappointment, and death, into blessings for the soul, — blessings of unearthly sweetness, and a virtue which nothing can touch, subsisting through every change into the eternal life. This discipline we learn from Him who has consecrated sorrow, and made death beautiful. The suffering Christ is the best supporter of the heart that is bowed with grief. He passed through all the crises of our humanity, even our doubts and our fears, and fathomed the darkest depths of sorrows. But the fear was momentary; the doubt only rose to pass away. Fear and doubt were alike dissolved in the warmth of that human love which prayed for enemies, and comforted the penitent, and consigned the weeping mother to the tried affection of the friend; — fear and doubt passed away in the clear visions of that heavenly trust which spoke forth triumphant in the words, "Father, into thy hands I commend my spirit."

CHRIST CARING FOR US.

NEW YORK OBSERVER.

"For he hath said, I will never leave thee, nor forsake thee." — HEB. xiii. 5.

I WILL never, never leave thee,
I will never thee forsake,
I will guide, and save, and keep thee,
For My name and mercy's sake.
Fear no evil,
Only all My counsel take.

When the storm is raging round thee,
Call on Me in humble prayer;
I will fold My arms about thee,
Guard thee with the tenderest care.
In the trial,
I will make thy pathway clear.

When thy sky above is glowing,
And around thee all is bright,
Pleasure like a river flowing,
All things tending to delight,
I 'll be with thee;
I will guide thy steps aright.

When thy soul is dark and clouded,
Filled with doubt and grief and care,
Through the mists by which 't is shrouded
I will make a light appear,
And the banner
Of my love I will uprear.

Thou mayst leave my care and keeping;
Thou mayst wander far from me;
Sorrow, then, and woe, and weeping,
Mercy must mete out to thee;
To the righteous
My rich blessings all are free.

When thy feeble flame is dying,
And thy soul about to soar
To that land where pain and sighing
Shall be heard and known no more,
I will teach thee
To rejoice that life is o'er.

"Come, and let us return unto the Lord; for he hath torn, and he will heal us; he hath smitten, and he will bind us up." — HOSEA vi.

"In my distress I cried unto the Lord, and he heard me." — PSALM CXX.

CONSOLATORY EPISTLE TO A BEREAVED DAUGHTER.

REV. W. F. WILLIAMS.

AGAIN you have followed a near relative to the grave. You have seen your father, like a shock of corn fully ripe, go down to his rest in peace.

"Asleep in Jesus! blessed sleep!
From which none ever wake to weep."

And I rejoice with you! Yes, it is, at least it should be, to you a matter of joy, profound and unutterable thankfulness, that should cause your full, welling heart to overflow with grateful praise. Grief becomes not a Christian in such a case. Nay, it is a grievous sin that should be repented of. See how many reasons for joy you have.

I. God did it. That should, at least, sweeten the bitterest cup,—should tinge with joy the saddest, most painful, the most unmitigated bereavement. He not only doeth all things well, but at the right and the very best time. If no other ray gilds the blackness of the storm, this shines in upon the soul and answers peace. This must hush throbbings of tumultuous grief; but,

II. You have hope—nay, shall I not say, certainty?—in his death. Some die as they have lived,—"having no hope and without God in the world." Have you ever tried to imagine what it would be to drink *such* a cup of affliction, of bereavement? To feel almost sure that a dear friend was lost! Some have even this to quaff, and yet it becomes to them of "the all things which work together for good." The number is larger who are called to follow very dear friends to the grave, of whom they indeed have hope, but staggered by some painful, oppressive doubts. You have assuring hope in his death. Why, then, should you weep? You believe him to be now tasting of joys infinitely beyond any he ever conceived! To mourn is selfish.

III. He had filled out his days, and has gone to his reward. "The days of the years of our pilgrimage are threescore years and ten, and if by reason of strength they be fourscore, yet is their strength labor and vanity, for it is soon cut off."

When your brother was taken, you felt that, though God did it wisely and well, and though you had hope in his death, he was cut off in the midst of his days, — at the threshold of his usefulness; and there was a painful sense of unaccomplished good, of an unfulfilled mission, of unemployed preparations, of a future cut off and extinguished; and the heart will busy itself with such things, whether it has a right to or not. But here the work is done, the summer is past, the day is ended; why should not the sun set? Would you have it ever halting upon the horizon? Shall it shine upon no other lands? Having ceased here from labor, shall he not enter into his rest?

IV. There is nothing to call for his stay. He has lived to see his family grow up and settle into their places in the world. None are longer dependent upon him, and there is not a reason for wishing him to stay, except the selfish one of desiring a little longer the luxury of his society, — and would you, for this, when his labors are ended and reward ready, would you, for this, keep him from the celestial city, the pearly gates? Nay, dry thy tears and break forth into jubilant strains, that another weary pilgrim has crossed safely the narrow stream, and entered into eternal rest, — rest, — rest, — rest. No more heat, nor weariness, nor toil, nor cold, — *no more sin.* O soon, soon we shall be there, — soon, too, our weary way will be over! Let us buckle up our harness, tighten our girdle, grasp our staff and press on, — press on, the little weary way before us. The Lord give us grace to be faithful every day, every hour, to every duty as it comes up!

ON THE DEATH OF AN AGED FATHER.

H. W. Rockwell.

How still he lies upon his funeral bier, —
  His pale hands clasped, and that bold, manly brow,
And honest face, that beamed for fourscore years
  With constant sunshine, cold and lifeless now!
Well may ye weep, and in the dust be bowed,
For ye are passing now "beneath the cloud."

Go! bear him gently to his clay-cold bed,
  And shed your tears like drops of April rain!
Ay! look your last upon his coffined head!
  For he will wake no more on earth again!
The fallen tree must lie where it is cast,
But death will spare the memory of the past.

His life was pure and gentle, and there shone
  A kindly summer ever in his eye,
Nor did the outcast, or the abject one,
  Look for a friend in vain while he was nigh;
He would have given the poor man half his store,
Rather than send him hungry from his door.

The lengthening shadows of a green old age
  Stole peacefully upon him, day by day,
And virtues no one saw gave life's fair page
  A freshness which survives the heart's decay:
And so at last, as he had lived, he went
To reap the promise of a life well spent.

'T is meet that in the evening of his days
  He thus should pass from us to his reward!
When the heart falters and the frame decays,
  It is not death, but life, that seemeth hard,
And long the spirit sighs beneath its load,
To join the blessed in their serene abode.

"O death, how sweet thy remembrance to the aged pilgrim who has never been satisfied with the world, and who is already, in this life, so borne up and elevated by the promises of eternal life as to say, 'I fear not thy scythe, — it cuts only that which I willingly leave behind, that I may be borne yonder, without encumbrance, on the wings of the spirit!' Yes, to him who has the Saviour, old age changes so imperceptibly its setting sun into the dawn of day, that night can scarcely be thought to lie between." — Dr. Tholuck's Hours of Christian Devotion.

"The dust shall return to the earth as it was: and the spirit shall return unto God who gave it." — Ecclesiastes xii.

DEPARTED SAINTS.

Doctor Newman.

They are at rest:
We may not stir the heaven of their repose
By rude invoking voice, or prayer addrest
  In waywardness to those,
Who in the mountain grots of Eden lie,
And hear the fourfold river as it murmurs by.

They hear it sweep
In distance down the dark and savage vale;
But they at rocky bed, or current deep,
Shall never more grow pale;
They hear, and meekly muse, as fain to know
How long untired, unspent, that giant stream shall flow.

And soothing sounds
Blend with the neighboring waters as they glide;
Posted along the haunted garden's bounds,
Angelic forms abide,
Echoing, as words of watch, o'er lawn and grove,
The verses of that hymn which seraphs chant above.

THE HEAVENLY LAND.

FROM THE GERMAN OF UHLAND.

THERE is a land where beauty will not fade,
Nor sorrow dim the eye;
Where true hearts will not shrink nor be dismayed,
And love will never die.
Tell me,—I fain would go,
For I am burdened with a heavy woe;
The beautiful have left me all alone;
The true, the tender from my path have gone;
And I am weak, and fainting with despair;
Where is it? Tell me where!

Friend, thou must trust in Him who trod before
  The desolate paths of life;
Must bear in meekness, as he meekly bore,
  Sorrow, and toil, and strife.
Think how the Son of God
These thorny paths hath trod;
Think how he longed to go,
Yet tarried out for thee the appointed woe;
Think of his loneliness in places dim,
When no man comforted nor cared for him;
Think how he prayed, unaided and alone,
In that dread agony, "Thy will be done!"
Friend, do not then despair:
Christ, in his heaven of heavens, will hear thy prayer.

THE UNVEILED DEALINGS.

The Words of Jesus.

"Remember the words of the Lord Jesus, how he said,"—"What I do, thou knowest not now; but thou shalt know hereafter."—John xiii. 7.

O blessed day, when the long-sealed book of mystery shall be unfolded, when the "fountains of the great deep shall be broken up," "the channels of the waters seen," and *all* discovered to be one vast revelation of unerring wisdom and ineffable love! Here we are often baffled at the Lord's dispensations; we cannot fathom his ways;—like the well of Sychar, they are deep, and we have nothing to draw with. But soon the "mystery of God will be finished"; the enigmatical "seals," with all their inner meanings opened. When that "morning without clouds" shall break, each soul will be like the angel standing in the sun, — there will be no shadow; all will be perfect day!

Believer, be still! The dealings of thy Heavenly Father may seem dark to thee; there may seem now to be no golden fringe, no "bright light in the clouds"; but a day of disclosure is at hand. "Take it on trust a little while." An earthly child takes *on trust* what his father tells him: when he reaches maturity, much that was baffling to his infant comprehension is explained. Thou art in this world in the nonage of thy being. Eternity is the soul's immortal manhood. *There*, every dealing will be vindicated. It will lose all its "darkness" when bathed in the floods "of the excellent glory."

"My thoughts are not your thoughts, neither are your ways my ways, saith the Lord." — ISAIAH lv.

"For we know that if our earthly house of this tabernacle were dissolved, we have a building of God, a house not made with hands, eternal in the heavens." — 2 CORINTHIANS v.

HEAVEN A CHARACTER, AND NOT A LOCALITY.

THOMAS CHALMERS, D.D., LL.D.

THE character wherewith we sink into the grave at death, is the very character wherewith we shall reappear on the day of resurrection. The character which habit has fixed and strengthened through life adheres, it would seem, to the disembodied spirit, through the mysterious interval which separates the day of our dissolution from the day of our account,— when it will again stand forth, the very image and substance of what it was, to the inspection of the Judge and the awards of the judgment-seat. The moral lineaments which be graven on the tablet of the inner man, and which every day of an unconverted life makes deeper and more indelible than before, will retain the very impress they have gotten,— unaltered and uneffaced, by the transition from our present to our future state of existence. There will be a dissolution, and then a reconstruction of the body, from the sepulchral dust into which it had mouldered. But there will be neither a dissolution nor a renovation of the spirit, which, indestructible both in character and essence, will weather and retain its identity, on the midway passage between this world and the next, so that at the time of quitting its earthly tenament we may say, that, if unjust now, it will be unjust still; if righteous now, it will be righteous still; and if holy now, it will be holy still. . . . . .

There may be palms of triumph; there may be crowns of unfading lustre; there may be pavements of emerald, and rivers of pleasure, and groves of surpassing loveliness, and palaces of delight, and high arches in heaven which ring with sweetest melody; but, mainly and essentially, it is a moral glory which is lighted up there; it is virtue which blooms and is immortal there; it is the goodness by which the spirits of the holy are regulated here,—it is this which forms the beatitude of eternity. The righteous now, who, when they die and rise again, shall be righteous still, have heaven already in their bosoms; and when they enter within its portals, they carry the very being and substance of its blessedness along with them, — the character, which is itself the whole of heaven's worth, the character, which is the very essence of heaven's enjoyments. . . . . There is no sound and Scriptural Christian who ever thinks of virtue as the price of heaven. It is something a great deal higher, — it is heaven itself, — the very essence of heaven's blessedness. For heaven is not so much a locality as a character.

"The dust shall return to the earth as it was; and the spirit shall return unto God who gave it." — ECCLESIASTES xii.

"I will not fail thee nor forsake thee. Be strong and of a good courage." — JOSHUA i.

HOUSEHOLD SORROW.

KNICKERBOCKER MAGAZINE.

A SHADOW broods over the household,
  A shadow still and deep;
I feel its presence around my heart
  Like a thrill of suffering creep.

It hushes the baby's laughing voice,
  Though the child can dream not why;
But the half-smile dies on its rosy lip,
  And wonder fills its eye.

I look far out in the sunshine,
  That bathes the earth in light;
And the voice of Nature murmureth low
  Her manifold delight.

But the shadow, — oh! close it falleth
  Through the dim and dusky air,
And we whisper low, and with light footfall
  We press the echoing stair.

And yet so soundly she sleeps alone,
  In that chamber cold and dim;
No noise from this busy world without
  Can reach her world within.

The shadow cast from the old pine-tree
  Flickers upon her face,
Mocking the play of the features, rare
  In their pure and chiselled grace.

And the wind stirreth tresses long and brown, —
  'T is but the wind alone;
Sad tears are filling our eyes to see
  How stilly she sleepeth on.

The sorrow that broods o'er the household
  Marks every weary brow;
Hers only is quiet and peaceful, —
  She heedeth no sorrow now; —

She whose warm heart felt ever
  The woes of other hearts, —

Whose sympathizing eye would draw
The sting of suffering's darts.

The shadow over the household,
The shadow from Death's pale wing,
Shall fill our souls with anguish
Of a lifelong suffering.

GOD MUST BE ACKNOWLEDGED, AND SUBMITTED TO IN ALL OUR AFFLICTIONS.

JOHN OWEN, D.D.

THERE is in many afflictions something that seems *new and peculiar*, with which the soul is surprised, and in which it cannot readily reduce its condition to what is taught about afflictions in general. This perplexes and entangles it. It is not affliction it is troubled with, but some one thing or other in it that appears with an especial dread to the soul, so that it questions whether ever it were so with any other, and is thereby deprived of the support which from former examples it might receive. And, indeed, when God intends a deep affliction, he will put an edge upon it, in matter, or manner, or circumstances, that shall make the soul feel its sharpness; he will not be governed by our bounds and measures with which we think we could be content; but he will put the impress of his own greatness and terror upon it, that he may be acknowledged and submitted to. Such was the state with Naomi, when, from a full and plentiful condition, she went into a strange country with a husband and two sons, where they all died leaving her destitute and poor. Hence, in her account of God's dealings with her, she says, "Call me not Naomi," that is, pleasant, "but call me Mara," that is, bitter, "for the Almighty hath dealt very bitterly with me."

"No chastening for the present seemeth to be joyous, but grievous; nevertheless, afterward it yieldeth the peaceable fruit of righteousness unto them which are exercised thereby." — HEBREWS xii.

"Surely He hath borne our griefs, and carried our sorrows." — ISAIAH liii.

THE MEETING PLACE.

DR. H. BONAR.

"The ransomed of the Lord shall return and come to Zion with songs and everlasting joy upon their heads." — ISAIAH XXXV.

WHERE the faded flower shall freshen, —
  Freshen never more to fade;
Where the shaded sky shall brighten, —
  Brighten never more to shade;
Where the sun-blaze never scorches;
  Where the star-beams cease to chill;
Where no tempest stirs the echoes
  Of the wood, or wave, or hill;
Where the morn shall wake in gladness,
  And the noon the joy prolong,

Where the daylight dies in fragrance,
'Mid the burst of holy song;—
Brother, we shall meet and rest,
'Mid the holy and the blest!

Where no shadow shall bewilder,
Where life's vain parade is o'er,
Where the sleep of sin is broken,
And the dreamer dreams no more;
Where the bond is never severed,—
Partings, claspings, sob and moan,
Midnight waking, twilight weeping,
Heavy noontide,—all are done;
Where the child has found its mother,
Where the mother finds the child;
Where dear families are gathered
That were scattered on the wild;—
Brother, we shall meet and rest,
'Mid the holy and the blest!

Where the hidden wound is healed,
Where the blighted life reblooms,
Where the smitten heart the freshness
Of its buoyant youth resumes;
Where the love that here we lavish
On the withering leaves of time,
Shall have fadeless flowers to fix on,
In an ever spring-bright clime;
Where we find the joy of loving
As we never loved before,—
Loving on, unchilled, unhindered,
Loving once and evermore;—

Brother, we shall meet and rest,
'Mid the holy and the blest!

Where a blasted world shall brighten
Underneath a bluer sphere,
And a softer, gentler sunshine
Shed its healing splendor here;
Where Earth's barren vales shall blossom,
Putting on her robe of green,
And a purer, fairer Eden
Be where only wastes have been;
Where a King in kingly glory,
Such as earth has never known,
Shall assume the righteous sceptre,
Claim and wear the holy crown;—
Brother, we shall meet and rest,
'Mid the holy and the blest!

SEEK HOLINESS RATHER THAN CONSOLATION.

THOMAS C. UPHAM.

OUT of death springs life. We must die naturally, in order that we may live spiritually. The beautiful flowers spring up from dead seeds; and from the death of those evil principles, that spread so diffusively and darkly over the natural heart, springs up the beauty of a new life, the quiet but ravishing bloom of holiness. Seek holiness rather than consolation. Not that consolation is to be despised, or thought light of; but solid, permanent consolation is the result rather than the forerunner of holiness; therefore he who seeks consolation as a distinct and independent object, will miss it. Seek and possess holiness, and consolation (not, perhaps, often in the form of ecstatic and rapturous joys, but rather of solid and delightful peace) will follow as assuredly as warmth follows the dispensation of the rays of the sun. HE WHO IS HOLY MUST BE HAPPY.

"We must through much tribulation enter the kingdom of God." — ACTS xiv.

"Fear not: believe only." — LUKE viii.

THE CLOUDLESS.

LONDON QUARTERLY.

"Sorrow and sighing shall flee away." — ISAIAH xxxv. 10.

No shadows yonder!
All light and song:
Each day I wonder,
And say, How long
Shall time me sunder
From that dear throng?

No weeping yonder!
All fled away,

While here I wander
  Each weary day,
And sigh as I ponder
  My long, long stay.

No parting yonder!
  Time and space never
Again shall sunder;
  Hearts cannot sever;
Dearer and fonder
  Hands clasp for ever.

None wanting yonder!
  Bought by the Lamb;
All gathered under
  The evergreen palm;
Loud as night's thunder
  Ascends the glad psalm.

aven is a day without a cloud to darken it, and without a night to ..id it." — J. Mason.

"Jesus reigns, the Life, the Sun
  Of that wondrous world above;
All the clouds and storms are gone,
  All is light and all is love.
All the shadows melt away
In the blaze of perfect day!" — Lange.

RESURRECTION.

KLOPSTOCK.

"This corruptible must put on incorruption, and this mortal must put on immortality." — 1 CORINTHIANS xv. 53.

THOU shalt arise! my dust, thou shalt arise!
Not always closed thine eyes;
    Thy life's first Giver
    Will give thee life for ever.
        Ah, praise His name!

Sown in darkness but to bloom again
When, after winter's reign,
    Jesus is reaping
    The seed now quietly sleeping.
        Ah, praise His name!

Day of praise; for thee, thou wondrous day,
In my quiet grave I stay;
    And when I number
    My days and nights of slumber,
        Thou wakest me!

Then, as they who dream, we shall arise
With Jesus to the skies,
    And find that morrow,
    The weary pilgrim's sorrow,
        All past and gone!

Then within the Holiest I tread,
By my Redeemer led,
Through heaven soaring,
His holy name adoring.
Eternally!

A JOYFUL RESURRECTION.

THE FAITHFUL PROMISE.

AT death the soul's bliss is perfect in kind; but this bliss is not complete in degree, until reunited to the tabernacle it has left behind to mingle with the sods of the valley. But tread lightly on that grave; it contains precious, because ransomed dust! My body, as well as my spirit, was included in the redemption price of Calvary; and "them also which sleep in Jesus will God bring with him." O blessed jubilee-day of creation, when Christ's "dead men shall arise"; — when, together with His dead body, they shall come; and the summons shall sound forth, "Awake, and sing, ye that dwell in the dust!" All the joys of that resurrection morn we cannot tell; but its chief glory we *do* know: — "When He shall appear, we shall be like Him; for we shall see Him as He is." Like Him! — My soul, art thou waiting this manifestation of the sons of God? Like Him! — Hast thou caught up any faint resemblance to that all-glorious image? Having this hope in thee, art thou purifying thyself, even as He is pure? Be much with Jesus now, that thou mayest exult in meeting him hereafter. Thus taking him as thy guide and portion in life, thou mayest lay thee down in thy dark and noisome cell, and look forward with triumphant hope to the dawn of a resurrection morn, saying, "What time I awake, I am still with Thee."

"Now is Christ risen from the dead, and become the first fruits of them that slept." — 1 CORINTHIANS XV.

THE VOICEFUL LAND.

REV. C. H. A. BULKLEY.

"Into the Silent Land!
Ah! who shall lead us thither?"

'T IS not a Silent Land!
Tones of harmonic spheres,
Heard not by mortal ears,
Thither their echoes roll
Into the answering soul:
O, 't is a Voiceful Land!

'T is not a Silent Land!
Voices of angel-throngs
Rain down their chorus-songs
Over ethereal hills,
Till the rapt spirit thrills:
O, 't is a Voiceful Land!

'T is not a Silent Land!
Harps with their golden strings,
Dipped, as in music-springs,
Swept by the touch of love,
Ring in the realms above:
O, 't is a Voiceful Land!

'T is not a Silent Land!
Footsteps of spirits sound
All through the air profound,
Gently as wind-tones make
Ripples on stream and lake:
O, 't is a Voiceful Land!

'T is not a Silent Land!
Ever celestial wings,
Bathed in the amber-springs
Deep of God's ocean light,
Fan the swift paths of flight:
O, 't is a Voiceful Land!

'T is not a Silent Land!
Psalm-breaths of joy arise,
Pulsing through inner skies,
When the sin-child returns
Whither truth's incense burns:
O, 't is a Voiceful Land!

'T is not a Silent Land!
Hosts of the pure and true
Shouts of delight renew

Round the beloved, fled
Far from the speechless dead:
O, 't is a Voiceful Land!

'T is not a Silent Land!
Welcomes divine are given,
Whene'er death's fetter 's riven,
Holy ones evermore
Step on the better shore:
O, 't is a Voiceful Land!

'T is not a Silent Land!
Far from the song-wrapt throne
Peals the unchanging tone,
Keying all notes above
To the unisons of love:
O, 't is a Voiceful Land!

" Every Christian that goes before us from this world is a ransomed it, waiting to welcome us in heaven. Every gem which death rudely s away from us here, is a glorious jewel for ever shining there." — PRESIDENT EDWARDS.

IN MEMORIAM.

ALFRED TENNYSON.

I SOMETIMES hold it half a sin
  To put in words the grief I feel;
  For words, like nature, half reveal,
And half conceal, the soul within.

But for the unquiet heart and brain,
  A use in measured language lies;
  The sad mechanic exercise,
Like dull narcotics, numbing pain.

In words like weeds, I 'll wrap me o'er,
  Like coarsest clothes against the cold;
  But that large grief which these infold
Is given in outline and no more.

SUSPIRIA.

H. W. Longfellow.

Take them, O Death; and bear away
  Whatever thou canst call thine own:
Thine image stamped upon this clay
  Doth give thee that, but that alone.

Take them, O Grave; and let them lie
  Folded upon thy narrow shelves,
As garments by the soul laid by,
  And precious only to ourselves.

Take them, O great Eternity;
  Our little life is but a gust
That bends the branches of thy tree,
  And trails its blossoms in the dust.

www.ingramcontent.com/pod-product-compliance
Lightning Source LLC
LaVergne TN
LVHW020228110826
845151LV00003B/851

* 9 7 8 1 4 2 5 5 3 2 8 0 2 *